THE OUTRAGEOUS IDEA OF
ACADEMIC FAITHFULNESS

DONALD OPITZ
AND DEREK MELLEBY

Brazos Press
Grand Rapids, Michigan

Published by Brazos Press
a division of Baker Publishing Group
P.O. Box 6287, Grand Rapids, MI 49516-6287
www.brazospress.com

Printed in the United States of America

Library of Congress Cataloging-in-Publication Data
Opitz, Donald, 1960–
    The outrageous idea of academic faithfulness / Donald Opitz and Derek Melleby.
      p. cm.
    Includes bibliographical references.
    ISBN 10: 1-58743-210-2 (pbk.)
    ISBN 978-1-58743-210-1 (pbk.)
    1. Christian college students—Religious life. I. Melleby, Derek, 1977– II. Title
BV4531.3.O65 2007
248.8′34—dc22   2006101734

13 14 15 16   11 10 9 8 7 6

CONTENTS

ACKNOWLEDGMENTS

Gratitude is best expressed in person, but a brief word in print is also due here. Thank you to these friends who have contributed their expertise and encouragement—Byron Borger, Walt Mueller, Chris and Jane Klein, Suhail Hanna, and Bill Romanowski. We are also grateful for the guidance and assistance of the team at Brazos Press—Rodney Clapp, Rebecca Cooper, and Jeremy Wells. We've received input from dozens of students in the course of writing this book, and the words of a few are recorded within: Christie Gustafson, Erin Lichti, Mike Master, Brea McCauley, and Molly Metcalf. And finally, thank you to our wives, Christine and Heidi, for putting up with us and (occasionally) laughing at our jokes. Our gratitude is immeasurable.

INTRODUCTION

This book is the effort of two friends whose friendship was forged in large measure by the shared concerns expressed on these pages. Many voices other than our own are inked here—students, colleagues in campus ministry, and authors we have never even met. Our hope is that these voices will come together for you as an invitation to an adventure. This is an invitation that we received in college—an adventure that we both wish we would have taken up from the start.

This book isn't a map or a guidebook that can lead you from the beginning of the journey all the way to its end. The subject matter explored here is too rich, too deep, and too personal to be mapped. It is more like a sign staked in your life to point you toward this adventure that we are calling *academic faithfulness*. It is a collection of stories and suggestions that we have found helpful and that others have reported were helpful to them. Perhaps these testimonies will aid you in your journey of faith.

We hope you won't have to set out on this journey alone. We have discovered that deep engagement and lasting change come when a journey is taken with others. Some of you may have the opportunity to read this book with a friend or mentor or with a small group or a class, and you will be able to consider the challenges raised here together and to add your own stories to those told here. For those of you who are trekking solo, we want to invite you to our cyber-spot (www.academicfaithfulness.com) so that you have a forum for asking questions, discovering additional resources, and hearing about the adventures of others.

The title of our little book isn't altogether original. George Marsden, a prestigious historian, published a thin volume in 1997 entitled *The Outrageous Idea of Christian Scholarship*. In it Marsden picks up where his former work, the award-winning *The Soul of the American University*, left off. Dr. Marsden calls on Christian faculty to be more thoroughly Christian in their own research and writing, to integrate more intentionally their own work as professors with their life-directing Christian faith. We are amplifying his call to academic faithfulness because we are convinced that this is God's call not only to professors but to every Christian student. We are writing this book to invite students into the adventure of uniquely Christian and culturally relevant learning. We believe that Christians are all called to "take captive every thought and make it obedient to Christ" (2 Corinthians 10:5 NIV). This is the adventure: putting everything that we are and have in service of the King. And during college we have a special opportunity to offer him our learning.

We also piggy-backed on the Marsden title because we liked the word *outrageous* and wanted it in our title. Many professors will think that your desire to connect learning and faith is outrageous. Your friends, even your Christian friends, may see academic faithfulness as an eccentric, even outrageous concern. Once we begin to explore what academic faithfulness entails, we imagine that even you may feel that this is a bit outrageous. In our own experience, when the topic of *academic faithfulness* or *Christian scholarship* has been raised, Christian students often see the challenge as beyond them, as a task for the stout and the wise, for the uniquely gifted. We think *every* Christian student has been called by God to think faithfully about learning. That is why we are trying to explore the connection between these two words: Christian and student.

- Does God care about academics?
- What difference might being a Christian make for a college student?
- What does faithfulness look like in the classroom?
- What is a Christian perspective, and how does one go about developing one?

In what ways does the passionate worship of God that is so prevalent among some Christian students on campus relate to the academic tasks of writing papers, reading assignments, and working in the lab?

Not everyone is ready for *outrageous*, but we are convinced that Christian discipleship calls us to just that—to live under outrageous grace, to love freely and unexpectedly (outrageous!), to celebrate and enjoy with exuberant gratitude, and to suffer and serve without regret (how so?!). While you are in college, engaged in an academic calling, we are quite sure that your work should be somehow outrageous. Academic faithfulness is outrageous, and a few of you are already beginning to discern that this is the adventure you are looking for.

We should make clear at the start that the Christian life is about much more than academic faithfulness. This is just one aspect of life that is under the lordship of Jesus Christ. All of life falls under the lordship of Christ, so hearty Christian discipleship is actually multifaceted. As followers of Christ we should be seeking together to discern what faithfulness looks like in various aspects of our lives—in our involvement in the local church, our relationships with family and friends, our care for the needy and suffering, our various roles as citizens and stewards (financial and environmental), and our enjoyment of recreation and the arts. There is a lifetime of discipleship ahead as we seek to discern the various callings of God to us for life in his world. There is great joy in discovering that, in a Christian view, every life matters, that everyday life matters, and that we are not left without some sense of what really matters in life! Our hope is that once you begin to engage in this one aspect of discipleship, *academic faithfulness*, perhaps you will begin to engage more deeply in the pursuit of faithfulness in other aspects of life as well.

We are not suggesting that attention to academics should displace other disciplines of the Christian life like prayer or studying the Bible or fellowship. In fact, we are quite sure that little growth will take place apart from earnest prayer, searching the scriptures, regular worship, and deep dialogue with a mentor and peers. A great deal of Christian nurture leads nowhere, however, precisely because it is not addressing the issues of life. Like it or not, studying is presently a central issue in your life, so developing a Christian perspective on it is an important expression of faithfulness.

Is this book for you? While any thoughtful reader may benefit from it, we have written with a certain audience in mind. We are writing primarily for Christian students, specifically those that are at the tail end of high school or early in their college experience. This is a book for disciples. A disciple is a student, a learner, and discipleship is a lifelong role. Perhaps some of you are already disciples and you understand that all of life is to be redeemed in Christ, that he is Lord of all and has called us to be ambassadors, reconcilers, laborers, servants (the biblical metaphors abound). Perhaps you already sense that faith isn't merely part of life, a nice add-on, but the wellspring of life. This is our view, and we want to share the joy and richness of this view with you. We want you to find the deep satisfaction of pursuing your daily labors (for now, primarily attending classes and studying) as service to God. We want you to experience the unending challenge of exalting Christ as Lord of your thinking. We want you to begin now to imagine the application of your learning—your studies and plans and dreams—as an expression of love, or better yet, as a conduit for the love of God.

We've done a couple of things to keep the text of this book as readable as possible. The notes are collected together at the end of the book, and we don't cite them with footnotes throughout the text. At the end of each chapter we have included discussion questions to help you reflect on key ideas, ideally with other students. Even though the book has two authors, we've used "I" language in order to avoid confusion. Finally, while only a few students were named in the pages that follow, they speak for dozens of students that we have worked with during this project.

The outrageous idea of this book is that God cares about our academic work. God loves learning. In Colossians 2:3 we read that in Christ himself are "all the treasures of wisdom and knowledge." Christ is the very source of learning, and his disciples are the intended recipients of that wisdom and knowledge. As we learn in faith, not only will our own capacity for wonder and insight and love increase, but others will benefit as well. Keeping these two things—faith and learning—connected is the key.

Discussion Questions

1. When you think about bringing the two words together—academics and faithfulness—what comes to mind?
2. At this point, do you believe the outrageous idea of this book: that God cares about your academic work?
3. Why do you think some people would consider academic faithfulness to be an outrageous idea? Who do you have in mind, and why might they think this way?
4. What are the implications of 2 Corinthians 10:5 and Colossians 2:3 for your academic work?

WIDE-EYED

CHAPTER 1

I don't know what the raccoon was thinking. He sat unmoving on the road, wide eyes reflecting the headlights of our VW Jetta. My daughter was driving, a rookie on the stick and big-hearted for creatures wild. Katie veered hard, banged over a six-inch curb, and blew the right front tire. Katie and I sat there, wide-eyed. Now I know what the raccoon was thinking: *My life is over.*

I was wide-eyed on the first day of college. My life was over, the first stage anyway. Sitting on a mattress in my room, waiting for some roommate to arrive, I knew I was leaving a great deal behind—home, friends, routines, and, by degrees, my family. The fear was buried deep, somewhere behind my stomach, but the uncertainty rattled around in my head.

- Where is my life going?
- What kind of person will I be here?
- Where will I fit in?
- Who was that girl with the sunglasses and arms full of boxes?

I wasn't sure who my roommate was going to be, where to go for dinner, why I was at college, or that girl's name. I only knew that something exciting and a little terrifying was beginning. I wasn't frozen in the headlights, but I knew I was on an unfamiliar road. I was ready for something new, for the next stage in life, and I found that I was wide-eyed, not so much with fear or regret, but with anticipation.

Students come to college with all kinds of expectations about what it will be like. Some expect that it will be like high school, only without the stupid parts like homeroom and bathroom passes. I thought it would be more like basketball camp, since that was the only other time I'd ever been on a college campus. So I spent most of my first year in the gym. One college friend thought that college was a perpetual coffeehouse. He stayed up most nights playing his guitar, crooning red-eyed romantics. Expectations have profound implications on what we actually find at college, and there are two common expectations that shape the experience of many college students.

Beer and Circus

Let's call the first common expectation Beer and Circus. Once again we are borrowing a title from a book, this one by Murray Sperber. Many students come to college with expectations that come from watching countless movies like *Animal House, Back to School, Old School, American Pie 2* and hearing harrowing stories of kegs consumed, rules defied, and pleasures found. Life at many educational institutions would come to a grinding halt if the lubricant of alcohol disappeared. Students aren't simply drowning in beer, however. The circus show that Sperber is most concerned about is college athletics, but there are many other things under the big top that also distract students from investing themselves in education.

Beer and Circus may state the expectation of incoming students too cynically. We could describe this expectation as Autonomy and Exploration, but that's not as easy to remember. The gist is the same, and the creed goes like this: "I am on my own, free of parental supervision and bogus limitations. I am here to make my own decisions about what I want to do and who I want to be." I'd have to admit that I began college with a good measure of this expectation.

Tom Wolfe provides a particularly poignant portrait of Beer and Circus college life in his recent book *I Am Charlotte Simmons: A Novel*. Young Charlotte begins college to forge her own identity. She quickly discovers that her professors are largely irrelevant and that the vast majority of her time and the powerful forces of identity formation come not from the curriculum, not from some program of academic exploration, but in the context of a student culture dominated by alcohol, sex, consumption (particularly of alcohol and sex), exploitation, and, consequently, cynicism. Poor Charlotte's identity is certainly shaped by her experiences. Unfortunately, the experiences are brutally painful. This is not a novel for the faint of heart. But then again, living in the pervasive culture of the American academy isn't for the faint of heart either. College will change your life forever, and many leave college with deep scars.

Beer and Circus runs pretty deep on campus, even in Christian *leaders* on campus. One beautiful April afternoon I got a call in my office. At the time, I was working in campus ministry out of a religious life office. Three of my friends, student leaders of a Christian fellowship group, thought that it was a good day to meet for tennis on the courts in the center of campus. I ran to my apartment to change and then across the quad to join my friends. As my friends came into view, I thought at first that they had found matching flesh-colored tights with fig leaves strategically attached. Weird, yes, but not entirely surprising for these three pranksters. As I walked onto the court, I finally realized that they were wearing shoes . . . nothing but shoes. Others playing tennis thought that this nude exhibition was hilarious, and a crowd soon gathered outside the fence. I thought the joke was on me and that once I stepped on the court they'd scamper to cover their pride with shorts, but I guess the sunshine felt too good. The show continued until my boss, the college chaplain, walked by on his way to a board meeting. I still laugh when I think about this story, even though this was certainly lewd behavior. Unfortunately, this wasn't the only expression of their vision of college life. For them, college was simply about making memories. It was Beer and Circus all the way.

Despite the clear biblical warning regarding drunkenness, I know of many Christian students who are "three sheets to the wind" most weekends. This is true even of many Bible and student ministry majors. One student, who was teaching a junior high school Sunday school class in a local evangelical congregation, recently excused his Sunday morning bleariness to his young students: "Sorry I'm not with it; I've got a huge hangover from last night's party." He lost his internship at that church the next day.

Beer and Circus isn't just about drinking and partying, however. It is about disengagement from the central purposes of higher education. Perhaps a bigger problem than alcohol on American campuses is a pervasive disengagement with learning. Many students skip classes, scorn assignments, and tolerate poor grades. They have given up on education. This happens for all kinds of reasons. One of those reasons is the appeal of the circus. There are all kinds of things to do other than study, and many of those things are enticing and readily available.

If you come to college with Beer and Circus expectations, your expectations can be fulfilled wherever you go to school. I imagine that you can play tennis *au naturale* at just about any school in the country, at least for a few minutes. You can also skip classes and endure the parental scorn of a few bad grades. If you come with the curious naiveté of a young Ms. Simmons, chances are good that the call of the barker and the smell of the peanuts will lure you to an entertaining show—an expensive circus to be sure.

Grades and Accolades

Some students expect something completely different. Let's call this expectation Grades and Accolades. These students may be hard-wired for curiosity, and they may find that an academic setting provides stimulating academic challenges. More often than not, however, these students aren't naturally academic overachievers. Their expectations have been shaped in the competitive forge of a dozen or more years of schooling, and they are often driven by the promise of the reward that comes to those who work hard. In the movies these students are portrayed either as nerds (often physics and computer majors) or as top-notch students (generally pre-med or pre-law) struggling to succeed but crushed by the weight of their parents' high standards.

Unlike Beer and Circus, Grades and Accolades does take studying seriously. The single-minded drive for achievement fosters an academic work ethic that is in some manner constructive. Academic achievement is not enough, however—not nearly enough. Academic success can become an idol. When an aspect of life (like success and grades or, as discussed in the previous section, fun and frolic) is raised up and given undue devotion, it becomes an idol. The idol of academic success may be widely praised and may hold out lucrative promises, but that only makes it more difficult to identify as an idol. It also makes it more difficult to despise. Spotting and despising idols is an important part of faithful Christian living. Being concerned about learning, even about grades, is appropriate, but too often students become obsessive about grades and success and begin to lose the bigger picture. Learning needs to be pursued with the right motives and applied to worthwhile purposes.

I once worked with a Grades and Accolades student, a literature major. Elizabeth (a.k.a. E) was brilliant, but the light mostly shined down, back into her books. She hadn't read everything in the world—that would be impossible—but it seemed like she had. And she didn't just read it, she seemed to understand it very well, and she could remember most of what she had read. I wouldn't say E had a photographic memory, but her ability to recall and even recite lengthy portions of literature, especially poetry, was astounding.

Let's play a little thought game with Elizabeth. And let's start by imagining an even better E, a super-clone we'll call E2. Now this E2 is everything that E is, but when it comes to academics she holds all abilities in perfection. E2 actually *has* read every piece of important literature in the world, and she has perfect recall of every word. And even more impossibly, she knows (somehow) precisely what each author intended by the words penned. E2 is beyond genius.

What would you make of E and E2 if you knew them? Would E2 make a better friend than the original E? Would she be more fun? More interesting? More responsible? I have no doubt that she could leverage her keen mind for a lucrative academic position and dominate *Jeopardy* until she grew bored with the meager competition. But would E2 be happier, and would her work please God more than the work of the mere mortal? While I think E2 would certainly be interesting, she is unlikely to be any more fun or loving or lovable than E. E2 could leap-frog ahead of every academic competitor, yet still she might realize that her life is fractured, her relationships strained, her character twisted, and her joy fleeting. Perhaps Grades and Accolades doesn't really provide what we most desire or need. Idols never do.

All for One

Some of my Christian friends would counsel both Elizabeths to give up their intellectual hunger and to find their satisfaction in Jesus Christ. They don't literally suggest burning secular texts in a huge bonfire, but they insinuate that single-minded devotion to Jesus leaves little room for academic dedication. These Christian friends might invite Charlotte Simmons and my sun-burned tennis partners to the bonfire as well. Let the liquor burn and every silly prank. Throw every distraction that keeps us from the goal into the flames. There is something to this willingness to forsake all for the gospel. Once you find the pearl, Jesus tells us, you can't help but give everything else away (Matthew 13:45–46). Jesus should matter above every other thing. Something needs to burn, but I don't think what needs to burn are really the books or even the beer.

Let's take another image of burning fire, and this one from Romans 12:1–2.

Therefore, I urge you, brothers, in view of God's mercy, to offer your bodies as living sacrifices, holy and pleasing to God—this is your spiritual act of worship. Do not conform any longer to the pattern of this world, but be transformed by the renewing of your mind.

In this passage Paul, the author of this important letter, takes us into the temple where sacrifices are offered before God. Animal sacrifices are the usual temple offering, but here Paul recommends a better offering—offer your whole self, not some token (like beer or money), not a part or a piece (like your mind or your spring break), but all of you. This is what real spirituality and real worship is about. It is a life on fire, offered up and given over to serving the one true God. This kind of life is not puffed up by academic arrogance, and it is not distracted by the circus. It is a life set on discerning God's intentions for his creation. And that is going to require, Paul tells us, the renewing of our minds.

Here, I think, is the central challenge of this passage: *don't conform; instead, be transformed.* This phrase would serve as a good academic credo. We could print it in Latin and place it on our seal.

Or we could spell out "be transformed" in Greek letters and print them on hoodies (the nice thick kind). Of course, some marketing gimmick isn't the real deal. Paul appears to be encouraging Christians to think differently, to live differently somehow.

Expectations matter, and ours need to be altered. We cannot simply conform to dominant cultural assumptions about college. We need to develop a view of higher education that has been deconstructed (de-idolized) and redeveloped—prayerfully, thoughtfully, graciously. In this we will be swimming against the strong current of a well-established collegiate culture. The power of the world that surrounds us, that rushes against us and flows within us, is more than considerable. Paul imagines that somehow we can swim upstream, that there is a power sufficient for our daily struggle. Is it possible, little fish that we are, that we can swim against these currents—

- a freedom-fixated, pleasure-seeking student culture
- the desire for self-advancement
- peer pressure
- the anti-intellectualism of our church traditions
- the secular assumptions of much of the academy

Paul thinks that we can, but only in Christ, and only together.

College wasn't what I expected. I thought that learning was going to be at the heart of the experience—classroom debate, late night philosophizing, engagement with important ideas. There was plenty of classroom debate, but mostly about grades. There were many late night conversations, but mostly about inane things. And of course I did encounter important ideas, but now I'm sad to report that I wasn't changed by those ideas as much as I had hoped. I don't mean to be cynical; it's just that for a year or two I lost interest. I was going through the motions, but I didn't care about my studies. Eventually something important did happen to me, but it happened late in college. I began to see things differently. And seeing differently made a world of difference.

Every student begins college wide-eyed, full of expectations. Some dream of the paradise of earthly delights, and others of the rewards of high achievement. Both of these dreams are ultimately disappointing, and it doesn't take too much soul-searching for students to discover that they want something more. Of course the yearning for deep meaning and for lasting purpose will never be discovered in the co-curriculum or even in the curriculum itself. The real answer is relational, personal, and more real than anything that can be imagined. The real answer is Jesus Christ. He is the one who is inviting us to renew our minds and transform our lives.

Discussion Questions

1. A few expectations that students have for college were suggested in this chapter. Summarize them in your own words.
2. What are/were your expectations for college? Where did your expectations come from?
3. What is an idol? What idols were mentioned in this chapter? What other idols are found (and worshipped) on college campuses?
4. Read Romans 12:1–2. What are the far-reaching implications of these verses for your time in college?

Recommendations

Donald Drew, *Letters to a Student* (Ross-shire, Scotland: Christian Focus Publications, 2003).

Kelly Monroe Kullberg, *Finding God Beyond Harvard: A Quest for Veritas* (Downers Grove, IL: InterVarsity Press, 2006).

BABYLON U

CHAPTER 2

Mrs. Burns shook the beans out of me. That's what my sixty-something kindergarten teacher with flaming red hair called it. I guess I was still trading my lunchbox snack when we were supposed to be practicing "quiet time." Burns was stealthy, and somehow she came up on me from behind and sank her talons into my shoulders. She shook so hard that I'm lucky my head didn't fly off. She wouldn't get away with this kind of abuse today, but back then we all fell prey to the talons at one time or another. And I guess we learned a lesson of some kind.

Evidently Robert Fulghum, author of *All I Really Need to Know I Learned in Kindergarten*, learned some lessons in kindergarten too, but all of his lessons are so sunny, so "Precious Moments." Here are a few of those precious lessons:

1. Share Everything.
2. Play Fair.
3. Don't hit people.
4. Put things back where you found them.
5. Say you're sorry when you hurt somebody.
6. Warm cookies and milk are good for you.
7. Take a nap every afternoon.
8. When you go out in the world, watch out for traffic, hold hands and stick together.

The lessons that I learned, reinforced by twelve more years of schooling, weren't so sunny:

1. Don't share, but strive to get ahead.
2. Cheat if you can get away with it.
3. Hit people hard, especially on the field.
4. When you find something, keep it.
5. If someone gets hurt, deflect the blame.
6. Cookies and milk may be good, but beer is better.
7. Sure, take a nap every afternoon, during chemistry.
8. When you go out into the world, watch out for perverts and look out for number one.

Maybe Fulghum went to better schools than I did. I don't mean to be so sour. I love school, and I loved just about every year of it. But I can't help feeling a little apprehensive about what is really going on. It sure feels like something is wrong in a setting in which violence and abuse is rampant, in which athletic prowess is celebrated more than academic achievement, and in which education for responsible action is easily trumped by education for upward mobility. Colleges and universities aren't what they should be either. In fact, nothing this side of Eden is as God intended. Sin has twisted and hardened each of us. Even human institutions like colleges and universities have been deformed by sin. Colleges are tangled in bureaucracy. The curriculum is fragmented and, as a whole, incoherent. I had no idea why I had to take half the courses I took, and no effort was made to show me connections between courses—or for that matter, the connection between coursework and life. Cultural idols like money and power corrupt the interests of institutional leaders and students alike. Academic ideologies mark fault lines between and within departments. Sometime during the first semester or so students come to this realization—*It's a jungle out there!* Most students will be able to skirt the quicksand of despair, but sooner or later all of us will be scratched and tangled in the nettles of a thousand conflicting ideas and values.

In an equally confusing world, Paul provided the Colossians with sage advice: "See to it that no one takes you captive through hollow and deceptive philosophy, which depends on human tradition and the basic principles of this world rather than on Christ" (Colossians 2:8). We need to recognize the danger of deceptive philosophies and traditions and to undertake our collegiate journey with care and courage.

Daniel and Friends

We can learn a great deal about surviving in the jungle of contemporary American higher education by studying a student born long ago and far away. The biblical prophet Daniel was born sometime late in the seventh century B.C. The northern kingdom of Israel had long before been taken into captivity by the Assyrians, and during Daniel's lifetime his own homeland of Judah too was sacked, this time by the Babylonians. Babylon was the most powerful nation of the world in that day. The Jewish people, vastly outnumbered and overpowered, could not stand up against the invading soldiers. Jerusalem was placed under siege and eventually was razed to the ground. There was one thin hope for the Jews—holding on to faithfulness as exiles in Babylon.

The Babylonian empire had spread quickly across what is today the Arabian Peninsula. In the process of rapid advancement the Babylonians learned an important lesson in ancient warfare—that every victory could not be followed by the annihilation of the conquered. Eventually the Babylonian armies would be depleted and spread too thin to maintain the regime. Some nations had to be conquered and left intact in order to enlarge the kingdom. Conquered nations would resume farming and trade and would pay tribute to the victorious empire.

This strategy for empire building worked particularly well for the Babylonians when the distinctive cultural identity of the conquered nation was dismantled and the people were enculturated into the new regime. Centuries later, Israel proved to be a constant thorn in the side of the mighty Roman Empire because the Jews refused to be assimilated. There is a lesson in this history, one repeated in dozens of contemporary movies: real heroes don't knuckle under. They stand for their own culture against the tyranny of invading colonizers.

The opening verses of Daniel reveal that a campaign to assimilate the Jews was already underway. Articles from the temple in Jerusalem were carried off to adorn the temple of a Babylonian god (v. 2). Young Jewish men, the best and the brightest, were also deported to Babylon (vv. 3–4). These young men were to be taught the language and literature of Babylon, and apparently they were to be spoiled in the process. Food from the king's chef and choice wine were provided. These students were also assured that important jobs in the Babylonian regime awaited them upon completion of their studies.

Why heap such generosities on these prisoners of war? King Nebuchadnezzar was killing two birds with one stone. At the same time that he was strengthening the administration of his kingdom with the best talent available, he was also subverting Jewish culture by removing key leaders and assimilating them into Babylonian culture. Pretty sneaky. Recruits were taught a new vocabulary and new stories and promised a better future. The new patterns of thought and life were affirmed and rewarded.

To be honest, such assimilation didn't just happen long ago in Babylon. Similar transformation happens for every student in a college setting. Students are confronted with new learning and stories, assured that lucrative employment awaits, and socialized into patterns of thought and life that may last with them for years to come. People are always being "trained" for certain patterns of life by the culture that surrounds them. What you learn and how you live while in college really matters. And to the degree that your mind is not renewed by the gospel and your life is not transformed by the power of Christ, you will conform to the dominant culture. (This takes us back to the earlier discussion of Romans 12:1–2, where we were encouraged to be nonconforming cultural transformers.)

Daniel and his three friends, Hananiah, Mishael, and Azariah, saw through the assimilation strategy. They chose to stay true to their own culture's dietary practices rather than to defile themselves with the royal food and wine. They convinced the official overseeing their "training" to let them eat only vegetables and drink only water for ten days. After ten days they looked healthier and better nourished than the other hostages, so the official let them maintain their diet. Perhaps this story about food is told because it reveals the first step in the faithful counter-strategy of the young Jewish men. Stay true in the little things, and trust in the provision of God.

Evidently these four young men were exceedingly sharp. The text tells us that to them God had given "knowledge and understanding of all kinds of literature and learning" (v. 17). Perhaps this came mystically, God pouring these insights into their ears at night. More likely these fellas were gifted with good minds and were provided with a good education. They were good students. Daniel was given a little something extra: the ability to understand visions and dreams of all kinds. When it came time for testing, the king himself questioned the hostage students. In every matter of wisdom and understanding these four tested *ten times* better than all the magicians and enchanters in the entire kingdom! Now I've scored well on a few tests in my day, but I don't think anyone would ever say that I was ten times smarter, even than a stone. Exaggeration or no, these guys were smart. And that's not the best thing about them. The best thing is that, come what may, no matter what, these guys were faithful. They stood up for what they believed.

Daniel chapter two sets up the memorable stories in chapters three and six. In chapter two Daniel's special gift for interpreting dreams comes in handy. None of Nebuchadnezzar's counselors or magicians was able to interpret the king's vexing dream. Nebuchadnezzar made the task tricky by refusing to relay the dream to them, so they couldn't rely on the usual hocus pocus and symbolic assessment. Failure to interpret the dream would spell disaster for the reputedly wise (v. 5). After much prayer, Daniel stepped forward and told the king both his dream and its meaning. This miraculous revelation elicited a good confession from Nebuchadnezzar: "Surely your God is the God of gods and the Lord of kings and revealer of mysteries, for you were able to reveal this mystery" (v. 47). Nebuchadnezzar was either a religious grandstander, or he was so religiously eclectic and confused that he could not live out this good confession. For all of his lavish praise of God, he had trouble staying true to his confessions. Daniel was, however, rewarded handsomely for his service to the king.

He was given fantastic gifts and placed in a position of high honor as ruler over all of Babylon's wise men and governor over the entire province of Babylon (vv. 48–49).

Daniel's first order of business was to hire his three friends to govern Babylon with him. Instead of staging midnight raids or plotting a subversive coup, instead of attacking Nebuchadnezzar and his policies, what did these four exiles do? They served in the empire that had destroyed their own nation and defiled the temple of God. These four Jewish lads enacted (as we will see) bold displays of peaceful resistance when the requirements placed on them required it, but in the meantime they applied their own wisdom to the cultural context in which God had placed them.

Faithful under Fire

When you've got more gold than you know what to do with, you can either (1) start another war to get more, or (2) build something really big with it. Nebuchadnezzar must have been growing tired of endless battles, so he resorted to the second option. On the plain of Dura, he erected a golden image of himself that was 90 feet high and 9 feet wide. It is no use making a gigantic idol unless people are going to worship it, so Nebuchadnezzar decreed that all people must fall down and worship the image of gold (Daniel 3:5). Hananiah, Mishael, and Azariah (renamed by the Babylonians as Shadrach, Meshach, and Abednego, another sneaky ploy to distance them from their own culture and beliefs and connect them to gods of Babylon) defied the call to worship this idol, even though the fiery furnace was super-heated and open wide to receive them.

Upon hearing of their defiance, Nebuchadnezzar was thrown into a rage. "What god will be able to save you from my hand?" The three friends took the opportunity to testify: "The God we serve is able to save us from the blazing furnace, and he will rescue us from your hand" (v. 17). They may have been shaking in their sandals, but you sure can't hear it in their words. In fact, the next line is delivered with such cool confidence that it almost sounds over-scripted. "But even if he does not, we want you to know, O king, that we will not serve your gods or worship the image of gold you have set up" (v. 18). Hananiah, Mishael, and Azariah were not about to be co-opted by Babylonian beliefs and laws. They would not conform, come what may.

In chapter six Daniel finds himself in a similar situation. Daniel, the text reveals, has excelled in unparalleled ways in all of his duties, and Nebuchadnezzar is ready to confer upon him the administrative oversight of the entire kingdom. In their jealousy, competing administrators conspire to discredit Daniel before the king, but they can find no corruption in him. Their diabolical minds don't rest until they hatch a plan to ruin Daniel. An evil envoy approaches the king and persuades him that the people want to dedicate themselves to a month of prayer for the king alone. They add a rider to this policy: anyone who violates this decree should be cast into the lion's den. When the feckless king went along with the plan, the trap was set for Daniel.

Daniel's response, like his friends before him, provides wonderful insight into the priorities, practices, and character of a faithful exile. Here is the text of Daniel 6:10:

> Now when Daniel learned that the decree had been published, he went home to his upstairs room where the windows opened toward Jerusalem. Three times a day he got down on his knees and prayed, giving thanks to his God, just as he had done before.

Daniel embodies for us not only courage but a deep commitment to faithful patterns of living. Come what may, he was going to be faithful.

Hananiah, Mishael, and Azariah were cast into the furnace, and Daniel into the lion's den. Obviously, faithfulness was risky business back then. Faithfulness is still risky business. I know two students who failed courses because their professors were annoyed by their desire to explore a Christian perspective on the subject matter. I know another student who worked to pay for another semester of school so he could take additional Bible and philosophy courses to equip him for his ongoing work in business. Many students have sacrificed glory on athletic fields for faithfulness in the classroom. And they have become outcasts on the party scene because they weren't willing to conform to that world. This certainly isn't the kind of sacrifice described in Hebrews 11. Some of the saints remembered there were tortured, imprisoned, stoned, and even sawed in two. But the sacrifices of these students were real nonetheless, and perhaps these are the kinds of sacrifices that we are being called to make.

Daniel and his friends were not simply faithful on the spot. They had been at it for a lifetime. Living faithfully in little things had surely prepared them for costlier sacrifice. And it had prepared them to live in exile. Though they served a culture not their own, the four friends were never enslaved by the idols and values of pagan Babylon. They lived in hope that one day they would serve a true king in an everlasting kingdom. In the meantime, when things got hot, they were joined by one "like a son of the gods" in the fire (3:25). And when things got wild, beastly wild, the tamer of all things wild was with them (6:22).

Panning for Gold

Life in America is a long way from life in Babylon. We could do much worse than to live in the cultural exile of our own day, but we must always keep in mind that life in a twisted world like ours is precarious and in many measures sinister. To one degree or another, every one of us has been *Babylonized*. We have been trained to fit into the dominant culture of our own day and to serve its gods. Simply being a Christian does not free one from bondage to cultural idols. We need to learn how to defy the idols of our culture while at the same time serving within our immediate cultural context. That's what Daniel and friends did. Obviously, it wasn't easy.

Education has played an important role in shaping us for this dominant culture. Schools and colleges shape us to think and live in certain ways, and reinforce in us particular hopes and aspirations and attitudes. Some of these characteristics and goals are not so bad, whereas others may be diametrically opposed to God's concerns for life in his world. We need to sift our educational experiences carefully, straining out dross and keeping the gold. As we grow in wisdom, we learn how to handle the pan, and we become better able to discern truth from lies. And this really ought to be a central purpose of our education—to grow in discernment and wisdom. *A discerning person keeps wisdom in view* (Proverbs 17:24 TNIV). A wise person knows how to sift. And in order to pan for gold, you've got to be knee deep in the water.

There is much to learn while in exile. Daniel and friends were good students of their time and context. We also have much to learn from our "Babylonian" friends and professors, from those whose learning is not rooted in faith in Christ. I have learned a great deal from professors and authors who are not Christian, and even from those who are anti-Christian. In fact, *pirating* the riches of pagan scholarship is a very old practice of Christian intellectuals. Important insights into the nature of the world, of human beings, and of every academic discipline are discovered by those who do not have a Christian perspective.

Simply pirating pagan insights is not enough, however, not nearly enough. Borrowed ideas need to be carefully critiqued and integrated within a Christian perspective. This is one of the fundamental challenges of Christian scholarship and one of the responsibilities that you now have as a Christian student. We will provide some recommendations for this process of re-appropriating secular learning into a Christian perspective in chapter four. But for now, this is the insight that we want to emphasize: humility must mark us deeply as we study, for *with humility comes wisdom* (Proverbs 11:2). It was once written that Moses was the most humble man to walk upon the earth. This same Moses was educated in all of the wisdom of the Egyptians, and apparently his secular training helped to equip him to shepherd Israel (Numbers 12:3; Acts 7:22). Like Daniel, Moses is a pretty good mentor for the Christian student.

Educational institutions are home to all kinds of deceptive philosophies, human traditions, and worldly principles (remember Colossians 2:8?). But educational institutions are also thick with opportunities for character formation and faith development. If God has given you the opportunity to pursue advanced learning, thank him daily as you renew your mind and grow in wisdom. Whatever kind of educational institution you are attending, we think that God is willing to work with you right there.

Our perplexing times require that we cling to Christ in all aspects of our lives. Only in him can we live and love and think faithfully. The renewal of our minds is exactly what he has in mind. But every once in awhile, if you are like me, you need to have the beans shaken out of you to awaken you to the challenge.

Discussion Questions

1. Toward the beginning of this chapter we say that "education for responsible action is easily trumped by education for upward mobility?" What is the difference?

2. Read Colossians 2:8 and 2 Corinthians 10:5 (mentioned in the introduction). How are these verses similar? How are they different? Why are they important to keep in mind while you are learning new things?

3. Review the first six chapters of Daniel. In what ways is the story of Daniel a good example of what it looks like to be a Christian college student?

4. We suggest that, to one degree or another, everyone of us has been "Babylonized." What are some examples?

5. Pursuing academic faithfulness will require sacrifice. What sacrifices do you think you will need to make?

6. Whatever kind of educational institution you are attending, whether it be a Christian or a "secular" college, we think that God is willing to work with you right there. Are the challenges to academic faithfulness the same, no matter what kind of institution you attend? How might they be different?

Recommendations

Gene Edward Veith, *Loving God with All Your Mind* (Wheaton, IL: Crossway, 2003).

Tremper Longman III, *NIV Application Commentary: Daniel* (Grand Rapids: Zondervan, 1999).

Norman Klassen and Jens Zimmermann, *The Passionate Intellect: Incarnational Humanism and the Future of University Education* (Grand Rapids: Baker Academic, 2006).

BELIEVING IS SEEING

CHAPTER 3

I just came back from a vacation with my wife and parents, a road trip in which we toured the great north woods of Michigan. The parks and scenic vistas were breathtaking. Someday you have to see the massive sand dunes at Sleeping Bear, the mineral-dyed cliffs of Pictured Rocks National Lakeshore, and the Eden-like beauty of Toquomenon Falls. Upon return, I tried to convey the beauty with words. I'm sure you believe me that these spots are beautiful, but only seeing them for yourself will make you a true believer.

Now this was a long drive for us, so of course there was plenty of time to talk away the miles. My faith intrigues and baffles my parents, so beliefs were a central theme in our conversations. Mom and Dad are curious about what I believe and always courteous as they explore the peculiarities of the Christian faith. Entry points into this conversation are sometimes surprising. The big question for one leg of the long drive was this: Do you think there is life elsewhere in the universe? Perhaps I should have given the truest and briefest answer to that question: "I have no idea." But I'm used to talking about things about which I know very little—I'm a professor!

So I mentioned that Billy Graham (a Christian, though no astrobiologist) believed that there was intelligent life elsewhere. I also mentioned that there was a scientific outfit established to explore this question, the SETI project. I was stalling. I wasn't sure how to answer the question. Some peculiar beliefs are much easier for me to set aside. Even though sensational magazines and videos try to milk the Bigfoot myth and the mystery of crop circles, the plausible confessions of meticulous pranksters makes me more than skeptical about these claims. But about extraterrestrial life I really know nothing. I have no reason to *believe* (a thousand B-grade movies don't make it so), and I have no reason to *doubt*. No one in the Bible even thinks to address this issue.

If you told me that you saw an ET, well, I'd have to hear your story. Initially, I'd be suspicious, a bit of a doubting Thomas. We all live in the Show Me state. Since you'd have a hard time showing me that alien (presumably, you won't have one locked in your pantry), I'd have to assess your telling. Is your story plausible, and do I believe it?

Wouldn't you know that I totally missed the point? My parents weren't really that interested in ETs. Their follow-up question, on the leg between Mackinaw City and Munising, got closer to home: "How do you make sense of the story of Adam and Eve and the fossil record of primitive man?" Truth be told, I felt about as well-equipped to answer this question as I had the last one. So once again I employed a classic professorial ploy—trouble the extremes. *On the one hand,* evolutionary theory is stretched well beyond the evidence and can't really account for all it claims. *On the other hand,* conservative Christians have often over-interpreted the Bible, taking far too literally things that were not intended to be taken literally. And so on. You've heard this kind of hedging before.

In my own muddled mind, I hold things to be true that don't necessarily dovetail nicely.

- I believe in a real, historical Adam and Eve.
- I believe in an ancient creation with numerous signs of development, including adaptation of various species.
- I believe in primitive humanoids.

I can and do believe these things, even though I do not have an eloquent theory that unifies these beliefs or that others might find persuasive. Unfortunately, the recent work on intelligent design doesn't help much with this sticky question about the relationship between Eve and the cave man.

Seeing may lead to believing, but on many issues we are blind. There isn't anything to see, and yet we still have to decide whether we believe or not. On such issues it is the believing that leads to seeing. I believe in germs and justice and gravity, not by sight but because I've heard about them, I see that others believe in them, and they make sense out of many of the things I have experienced. Many of our beliefs are just like this. Once we turn our attention to deep beliefs, the ones that ground the others and shape the contours of our lives, I think we will discover that ultimately believing, not seeing, comes first for everyone. Beliefs come first and shape the way we see everything else. Good students must be reflective about what they believe, for their beliefs will shape their learning in profound ways.

To state this more academically, our deepest beliefs are pre-scientific, non-verifiable assumptions about the world and life. In other words, we believe them without empirical proof, and final proof of them is impossible. What is a human being, and how are we to live? What is the nature of reality, where did it come from, and what is its destiny? These questions, not questions about ETs or cave men, are the crucial ones. Philosophers have wrestled with the big questions for thousands of years, and science and experience contribute insight, but in the final analysis we all "live out" tacit answers to such questions. The answers to these big questions, the assumptions about life and reality that we live out, are the foundations of our worldview and the scaffolding of our minds.

A Whirlwind Intro to Worldviews

The term *worldview* is showing up in almost every discipline in the academy, and it is now widely used in discussions about faith, philosophy, culture, and education. The word jumped into English from the German, *Weltanschauung*, and has become increasingly familiar in the last forty years. The history and development of the notion are discussed in other places, and that doesn't need to concern us here. What we need at this point is a working definition of *worldview* and an initial overview of the contours of a Christian worldview. Here are three definitions of *worldview* that experts have given:

- a commitment, a fundamental orientation of the heart, that can be expressed as a story or in a set of presuppositions
- a comprehensive framework of one's beliefs about things that function as a guide to life
- a vision of life and for life

A worldview is a set of spectacles through which we see everything. It is the perspective or perceptual framework out of which we think and talk and move in the world. Our worldview opens up ways of seeing, and it points our attention toward certain things. It sketches the contours of what is real and what really matters, and it provides instructions about how to go about living in that reality. In other words, worldviews *describe* for us the reality that we will experience, and they *prescribe* to us how we ought to live in that reality. Worldviews also *proscribe* certain possibilities; they blind their adherents and limit their understanding and appreciation of certain things.

Worldviews are more caught than taught, or perhaps we ought to say that worldviews are generally absorbed through ordinary socialization. We generally don't evaluate various worldviews and select the most ideal—like shopping for a new pair of jeans. Most people aren't critically attentive to their worldview, but instead they live out the one they are born into, and they live it out relatively unreflectively. Because worldviews are generally lived out without careful attention, it is misleading to make them sound too academic or philosophical. They are not carefully organized and neatly articulated like a systematic philosophy. Rather, they are patterns of shared thought and behavior that constitute the structures and dynamics of culture. Social institutions, including the media, carry our culture's dominant worldview. The messages carried by these institutions shape us from early in our lives and throughout each day. Consequently, questioning one's worldview is uncommon, tinkering with the deep assumptions is precarious, and being transformed to live according to a new vision of and for life is nigh unto impossible. (*Nigh,* I say, not impossible.)

So this is yet another tough challenge that we are laying on you—the challenge to reflect about the deepest beliefs of your life. It isn't easy to take off the spectacles through which we see the world and to take a look at those spectacles. But if you've got the wrong prescription, it is delightful to discover the glasses that will enable you to see well. On the day I walked out of the eye doctor's office with my new glasses, I was overwhelmed by the detail that I had been missing for many years. Trees looked five times more beautiful. That sound in the front of the classroom was my sixth-grade teacher writing on the blackboard. During college I discovered that learning about worldviews, coming to understand my own and those of others, was the key to making sense out of all of my studies.

Like Gestalt

The discovery of molecules and atoms in the nineteenth century led to experimentation in painting in the early twentieth. Pointillism, the application of thousands of tiny flecks of paint to the canvas, was pioneered by Georges Seurat. Up close, the points of paint in his works are evident. One would be hard-pressed to see what the painting was about by giving attention to the points. From afar, the images, say those of *Sunday Afternoon on the Island of the Grande Jatte,* come into focus. People don't see in pixels; they see complex wholes.

I still remember encountering the word *gestalt* in Psych 101 during my first year of college. It was one of those foreign words that I thought I might be able to use someday to impress somebody (like you). The word was made popular in the early twentieth century, and it means something like "apprehension of a unified whole."

This morning I found shards of glass on my basement floor, and the butt end of a light bulb nearby. My guess is that our mischievous cat knocked it from a shelf. If I'd never seen a light bulb before, I'd have had a tough time visually reconstructing the bulb from the shards of glass. A picture of the whole helped me understand the pieces.

If I paid careful attention, even the glass shards of the light bulb would suggest that they once fit together. The glass on the butt of the bulb would suggest that there was once a unity of glass and aluminum. The pieces point to a whole. Our academic work is generally a study of pieces, fragments of the whole. As we study the pieces—in the sciences, the arts, the humanities, and throughout the academy—we may discover shards of insight, hints of coherence, and inklings of deeper meaning. Parts point to the whole, a gestalt. As with *Sunday Afternoon on the Island of Grande Jatte,* we need to step back to see the whole picture in order to understand the parts in context.

Our apprehension of reality is splintered into a million fragments. Sometimes advanced education makes reality feel even more fragmented. It would help if we could see a picture of the whole, if we had a grasp of the grand story of reality. I've got good news for you. That is precisely what the Bible provides. Learning to see wholes or, to tease the phrase a little, *to see through the whole*, is really the first step in developing a biblical theology and a biblical worldview. We need to step back from the Bible, and before getting drawn into particular points and passages, we need to survey the territory. We need to apprehend the biblical gestalt.

C-F-R-C

A Christian worldview, or biblical gestalt, begins with belief in the Triune God and God's revelation in the Word. Christians should turn to this revelation of God to discover the fundamental contours of a Christian worldview.

The biblical story, penned by dozens of authors in various genres, spanning two millennia of history, really is a coherent story. It has been exceedingly helpful for me to envision the story line, not as a flat timeline full of events, but in the shape of the comedy wave. I don't mean that the Bible is funny, though there are occasions of playful writing and ironic teasing. This story is a comedy in the classic dramatic sense. It begins on a high note, the story plummets as a tragic twist is revealed, and eventually, the horror is overcome on the way to a happy ending. The broad strokes of the biblical story are *Creation*, *Fall*, *Redemption,* and *Consummation*—C-F-R-C.

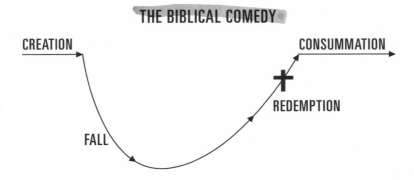

THE BIBLICAL COMEDY

CREATION

CONSUMMATION

REDEMPTION

FALL

The Bible is the story of God's own creation, the devastation visited upon that creation by sin, God's ongoing engagement with humankind to redeem that which has been befouled, and the eventual restoration of the entire creation in Christ. The Bible describes both humans and the world as good creations that came to be distorted by sin. Redemption is God's loving response to a world that has fallen under the destructive curse of sin. At the center of God's work of redemption, Jesus came as the redeemer of his church and of the whole creation. He came as the vanguard of the kingdom, as its ransom, and as its very king. Those who are followers of Jesus are called to carry on the redemptive love and activity of God. That's the story of the Bible in just six sentences. Of course there is so much more. For this story to become a worldview, we must learn to look through this story to see and respond to life in our own day.

A biblical worldview is a basic way of looking at all of reality from the perspective of the biblical story. It involves recognizing the structural goodness of the creation, that is, the creation itself is not the problem and was in fact designed to honor God. Human beings were designed to honor and obey God in this creational context, to develop the creation in ways that display God's good intentions. Because of our sin, however, our own lives have become full of confusion, pain, and self-interest, and the whole creation bears the marks of our disobedience. Nothing is as it should be, and we have all experienced the brokenness. All institutions are in need of the redemptive and restorative attention of Jesus and his followers.

The Bible provides us with basic principles for obedience, but it does not detail all of our responsibilities for the various areas of cultural activity. We need to work together to apply what we do know by Word and Spirit, and to seek to wrestle faithfully with what God might desire to see—in politics, sports, education, economics, marriage, urban planning, management theory, and so on. We know that we will not purge all evil and redeem the creation by our own feeble efforts. The glory of the renewed creation will finally be revealed when God judges and cleanses all things. Until that time, however, we participate in the work that has already begun in Christ.

While the creation was initially pristine and under the canopy of God's blessing, it was subjected to sin by our covenant representatives, Adam and Eve. East of Eden, after the fall, Adam and Eve parented a culture into existence. That sin-stained culture is manifest in Cain and his kin (Genesis 4). The history that we know and the cultures that we have inhabited are deeply marked by violence, chaos, and pain. This, however, is not the only world that Christians inhabit. In Christ, light came into the darkness; the kingdom of life invaded the domain of death. Jesus Christ is the firstborn of a new kingdom. Christians are living simultaneously in two cultures, in two kingdoms. They anticipate a coming day, however, in which God's restoration will be complete.

A Christian worldview provides a fundamental orientation to the nature of the world, to our own human nature, and to what is expected of us. It also ought to help us understand our place in history. We live in what has been called the "already and not yet" of the kingdom of God. In the coming of Jesus, the kingdom of God was inaugurated. This kingdom is the central teaching of Jesus. Even though the dominion of darkness surrounds us, we are assured that we have been rescued and repatriated into the kingdom of light (Colossians 1:13–14). Christians straddle two world orders. We are assured, however, that the creation will not always remain contested ground. One day the wicked will be judged, the creation will be cleansed, and the kingdom of God will be all in all.

Such a Christian worldview has extensive implications for higher education. Consider for a moment Jesus's parable of the weeds in Matthew 13:24–28.

Jesus told them another parable: "The kingdom of heaven is like a man who sowed good seed in his field.

But while everyone was sleeping, his enemy came and sowed weeds among the wheat, and went away. When the wheat sprouted and formed heads, then the weeds also appeared. "The owner's servants came to him and said, 'Sir, didn't you sow good seed in your field? Where then did the weeds come from?' "'An enemy did this,' he replied. "The servants asked him, 'Do you want us to go and pull them up?'"

In God's world there is much good wheat, but alas, weeds have been sown throughout the field by some enemy. This is exactly the situation we find ourselves in at college. We are surrounded by good things that God has provided, but everything is also overgrown and twisted. Discerning the wheat from the weeds—that's the challenge. Good bread will keep you going, but a belly full of weeds will make you sick and sorry.

Our dominant cultural worldview, modernity, has been influenced deeply by Christendom, to be sure, but it has also been shaped by beliefs that are alien to the testimony of scripture (modernity is both wheat and weeds). We need to work together to recognize sinister assumptions (like materialism), selfish cultural practices (like consumerism), and idolatrous ideologies (like nationalism) that have been woven into our own worldview. We all experience the conflict of living *east of Eden*, in a world twisted by sin. At the same time, those who are *in Christ* are beginning to taste the fruit of what might (and will someday) be, a world healed and fully restored by Christ. Many of us recognize that our own lives and our culture are not consistent with the desires of God and the message set forth in the Bible, but we are daunted by the challenge to change, and we are often uncertain about how to change. Most of our churches have not helped us develop our Christian beliefs into a worldview, a way of thinking about, living in, and challenging the world in which we live. No wonder so many of us have trouble thinking and living faithfully at college.

The challenge is huge. If you imagine that more than four years of mind renewal and life transformation will be required, you are absolutely right. But every Christian must wrestle with these issues, and college provides a great setting for the wrestling. Our culture's view of learning and knowledge is surely in need of some reform, and perhaps the resources of the Christian faith can point us in the right direction.

The Re-sighting of Saul/Paul

The Apostle Paul, while he was still known as Saul, saw the world in a certain way. His seeing was reinforced by years of academic training. Saul reflected upon and wrestled with his beliefs, and he was not content to believe privately. In fact, Saul was zealous in his beliefs. In Acts 9 Saul is in route to Damascus to ferret out Christian converts in order to capture (or kill) them. On this road Saul had an experience that changed him forever.

The light was blinding, and the voice was undeniably divine. "Saul, Saul, why do you persecute me? I am Jesus, whom you are persecuting." Saul discovered that he could not see, and those traveling with Saul were thrown into confusion. After the commotion settled, Saul's companions led him into Damascus, where he waited in darkness for three days.

The Lord was already at work across town. Ananias received a call, and though he resisted the Lord's rescue plan for Saul, he relented and found the house across town where Saul was waiting. Ananias placed his hands on Saul, and something like scales fell from Saul's eyes. After regaining his sight, Saul had to relearn how to see everything in terms of his dramatic encounter. Jesus had called out to him, Saul believed, and then his eyes were opened. Believing is not really seeing so much as being seen and then coming to see anew.

Saul was startled by the voice on the road, but he wasn't changed all at once. The miracles of being struck blind and then healed were just a nudge. In these events something new began in Saul, but it took years for him to change, years for him to become the Paul that we read in the New Testament. He was tutored by disciples in Damascus, spent three years studying somewhere in Arabia, and upon return to Damascus began preaching in the synagogue and debating local Jews. After a narrow escape from angry Jews in Damascus, Paul journeyed to Jerusalem to meet with the apostles.

Some of us had our eyes opened like this once. God acted, we reacted, and in a chain reaction everything began to change. But for me, for most of us, the change is slow, and we need lots of help along the way. In order to develop a Christian worldview and lifestyle, we will need to be discipled, to spend years of effort studying, and to begin to enact our new beliefs. As Paul discovered, doing so will lead to risk and adventure, suffering and joy.

Discussion Questions

1. We have suggested that "beliefs come first and shape the way we see everything else." What are some examples of things you believe without "seeing"?
2. Define "worldview" in your own words. How do social institutions, including the media, carry and perpetuate our culture's dominant worldview?

3. What do we mean by apprehending a "biblical gestalt"? Does your academic work feel like a study of pieces, fragments of the whole?
4. Read Colossians 1:13–14. What does this tell us about the contours of a Christian worldview? Kingdom is a central theme here. Is this a central theme of the Bible?
5. After meeting Jesus, Saul (later the Apostle Paul) had to relearn how to see everything in terms of his dramatic encounter. What are some things that you have had to relearn as you have grown in your faith?

Recommendations

Albert Wolters, *Creation Regained: Biblical Basics for a Reformational Worldview*, 2nd ed. (Grand Rapids: Eerdmans, 2005).

James Sire, *Naming the Elephant: Worldview as a Concept,* 4th ed. (Downers Grove, IL: InterVarsity Press, 2004).

Brian J. Walsh, J. Richard Middleton, *The Transforming Vision: Shaping a Christian World View* (Downers Grove, IL: InterVarsity Press, 1984).

A STORY-FRAMED LIFE

CHAPTER 4

A noisy storm was blowing into town. Our evening game of wiffle ball on the street was cut short, and we were trapped inside with the babysitter. My older sister Sharon and I had tied Marilyn up the last time she came to sit, so we didn't expect much trouble from her this time. This gave us plenty of freedom as we improvised the game from the street to make it more suitable as an indoor game. The bases outside gave us an idea for interior bases made of books. Soon every storybook we owned and every magazine in the house had been spread in every room as a complex maze of bases. We leaped from book to book, now more like stepping stones than bases. Soon little Debbie and Ted, younger still, joined the game. The booming thunder added one more dimension to the game. Every time the thunder clapped, we'd throw ourselves to the floor with a shout. There was an unexpected consequence to this rule—that night my brother and our dog both developed a fear of thunder that lasted for years.

Most people don't live jumping from story to story, but our lives are in significant ways based on one story or another. We can't really escape story. Each of us was born *once upon a time*, in a *setting*, surrounded by a *cast of characters*. The plot line of our individual stories rises and falls, twists and turns. Heroes and villains emerge; sometimes we are the scoundrel, sometimes the victim, and once in a blue moon, the hero. Most of our stories have romantic chapters (at least a page), accounts of mystery, an action sequence or two. I could go on and on about sweet Melissa (my romantic page), an unexplainable ball of fire (the mystery still haunts me), and being chased by thugs in a little town in Iowa. We've all got stories like these. The exciting parts are strung together by historical narrative, the mundane kind that is seldom recorded. *And on the eleventh day of October, I got up and ate a bowl of Mini-Wheats before heading to class. . . .*

While every story is unique in important ways, the similarities between our stories, at least the ones that emerge in a common cultural context, are remarkably similar. My story includes the same concern about comfort and security as the stories of my friends. My view of success and my desire for status is echoed in their stories. Not only do I want what my friends want, I even sound like them to a great degree. My biography is not as unique as I like to think it is. In fact, my story is enmeshed with the stories of so many others. This is another way to talk about worldviews. They are shared stories, and they arise out of the deep narrative of a culture. In the previous chapter we explored the notion of a worldview. The concepts and the illustrations in that chapter have been exceedingly helpful to us over the years, and we hope that those models will be helpful to you as well. However, the Bible is not really a model. It is a story—a massive, history-spanning epic. Finding our place in that story may help us understand our place in the academy.

Sometimes we need something startling, like a clap of thunder, to dislodge us from our limited biographies and to transplant us into a new story. Imagine how the story-frame of life changed for biblical characters like Abram and Sarai. One day they are minding their own business out there in Ur, just eating cereal or something. The next they are packing their bags, ready to begin a quest. Imagine that you are Moses tending sheep in Midian and you encounter—*can it be?*—a burning bush! Would your life ever be the same again? Peter probably thought he'd be fishing all day, and then again the next. Life before these encounters was story-framed, but the horizon of each story was limited—some valley in Ur, the desert of Midian, a seaside business. With the call, in the encounter, the frame of the story is stretched wide. Or to put it another way, these actors were cast into a new story. They became characters in the sweeping epic of God's love.

Evidently, God enjoys a good story. Otherwise, why create the glorious and pristine creation and then subject it to time and to human oversight? And isn't the Bible a story, the grand story of God's creation, its desolation, and its restoration? For the first ten years of my Christian life I read the Bible more like an encyclopedia than a story. I had questions, so I'd try to track down answers by using a concordance or some kind of Bible reference tool. This isn't so bad, but eventually good students of the Bible (and I'm still working on this) read the Bible as a story (nonfiction), and they enter into the epic adventure. With a great deal of reading and the guidance of wise friends and mentors, I eventually learned to interpret texts in context, to preach stories connected to The Story, and to consider academic disciplines as sub-plots of The Story.

Life in the Shire

Recently I led a Bible study at a local drug rehabilitation and counseling center. During one particular session, I was trying to communicate why we need to read the Bible and attend worship services. Desperately needing an illustration "on the fly," I shared with them how reading J. R. R. Tolkien's *The Lord of the Rings* helped me understand something about people in general and Christianity in particular. A few of the men had read Tolkien as teenagers and continued to re-read his stories while in prison, and all of the men had seen the movie, *The Fellowship of the Ring*. My illustration was well received and helped change their perceptions of the Bible.

Before explaining how I used Tolkien at the drug rehab Bible study, some personal background is needed. I had never read *The Lord of the Rings* trilogy as a child. (What kind of kid reads a thousand pages?) I knew of the books but never got into them. When the first movie was released in 2001, I was excited to see it. Many of my Christian friends couldn't stop talking about it. So I went and was disappointed. I couldn't get into it. I kept trying to over-analyze everything. What does the ring represent? Who are the Hobbits most like in today's world? Before I knew it, the movie was over and I had no idea what it was about! I was disappointed and confused, but I was determined to figure out why so many people loved these books. I purchased the trilogy and began to read. This time, however, I decided simply to read the books for what they were: fantasy stories, written by a very bright British fellow fifty years ago. This time I entered into the remarkable drama of Middle-earth (the setting of Tolkien's trilogy).

Back to the Bible study . . . I was trying to communicate the importance of Bible reading and worship. I drew a large circle on a dry erase board. This, I said, is Middle-earth. I drew a smaller circle inside of it. And this is the Shire, home of the Hobbits. "What kind of people are the Hobbits?" I asked. "Describe their characteristics and personalities."

The men proceeded to tell me that Hobbits were reserved, humble, not very adventurous, gift givers, and so on. "How are these qualities taught or reinforced?" I asked. This was more challenging at first, but eventually they understood what I was looking for: *Hobbits are Hobbits, to a large extent, because of the stories that they tell and the songs that they sing.* For example, Hobbits rarely leave the Shire because (1) they tell stories about the lavish goodness of the Shire, and (2) they tell terrifying stories about Hobbits who have left the Shire. Over time these stories have generated a particular attitude regarding leaving the Shire.

Now we were getting somewhere. You could see a few "lights" go on in the minds of the people in the room. I drew several more circles around the Shire and explained that the people in the surrounding communities also have stories and songs that develop, nurture, and shape people of that community. Moving away from Tolkien's story, I wrote "USA" in one of the surrounding circles. "What are some of the values of Americans?" I asked. This was easy for them: freedom, individualism, self-sufficiency, the American Dream. I didn't even have to make the connection. They started to tell me the stories that we tell and the songs that we sing that reflect these values. In the remaining smaller circles we began to put names of other cultures and had a great time pointing out the stories and songs of each.

And here is the point I was working so hard to drive home: As Christians, surrounded by so many competing stories and songs, it is vital that we gather at least once a week to tell the stories and sing the songs that make us a distinct people, the people of God. If we aren't nourished by these stories, chances are we will begin to live according to some other story.

Stories in Conflict

The biblical story (creation-fall-redemption-consummation) is in conflict with other life-framing stories. Two of these you will encounter throughout college: the grand stories of modernity and postmodernity. If you haven't encountered the notions of modernity or postmodernity yet, hold on, you will. These words describe not so much a clearly definable period of time (modernity running from 1500 to 2000; postmodernity still taking shape) as much as they describe something about the spirit and culture of Western societies. I guess you could say that these represent the dominant worldviews, or grand stories of the West. We can't explore these two tall tales in this brief book, but we thought that giving you a "heads up" about them was important.

Modernity has been the culture-shaping story of our time. It is not a story of creation, but of matter. It is not a story of the fall (of sin); it is the story of ignorance. It is not a story of redemption, but one of human progress. The story-frame of modernity (matter-ignorance-progress) is so compelling that most of us, even though we espouse the Christian story, live the tale of modernity. We have lived under modern assumptions for so long that they shape our thoughts and actions. We generally assume that

- The material is the real.
- Only the empirical can be truly known.
- Whatever is wrong (with me, with the world) can be righted by human insight.
- Eventually human beings will solve the problems of the world, and our technology will be the key.

These assumptions, this modern story line, has given rise to the academic culture of our day.

The American Dream is a romanticized version of this modern story. It goes something like this: The material world is stocked full of good things. This world is also full of restless consumers, and if we put our minds to it we can make lots of money so that we can move to a nicer home, buy a nicer car, and retire to a golf-course community. Many of you have seen your parents live this story. You've also seen that it's not all it's cracked up to be.

These days the story of postmodernity is becoming a best-seller as well. This story is being expressed throughout academic culture, popular culture, and even in the things we say to one another every day. In the classroom you may encounter deconstructionism and the politics of power, on the radio you will hear countless ballads of hopeless ennui, and in daily conversation you will hear the relativism of a culture that has given up on truth ("Well, that may be true for you"). The postmodern story begins not with creation or matter, but with culture. Rather than creation-fall-redemption (biblical) or matter-ignorance-progress (modernity), the story-frame of postmodernity is culture-oppression-expression. This story assumes that

- Reality is socially constructed, a human fabrication.
- Human beings can't help but to create realities that serve some and oppress others.
- There is no hope for ultimate healing, but at least we can strive to give voice to those who have been silenced.

The postmodernists are right that we live in a multicultured world, and it is certainly true that there are privileged groups and marginalized groups. To this extent postmodernity is instructive, and many of us are trying to learn to listen to the concerns of marginalized people. We don't want our privilege to be on the backs of others. So this story shouldn't be ignored. But in the end, like the story of modernity, this story isn't all it's cracked up to be either. The assumptions of postmodernity account for aspects of reality, but not the whole of reality.

Of course each of these three stories is nuanced, and different storytellers emphasize different parts of the story. The stories of modernity and of postmodernity provide helpful insights. They contain bits of truth. But as the meta-story, as the deep story that plumbs the depths of reality and of our identity, these are simply fractured fairy tales.

As Christian students we must be vigilant. Care must be taken when a chapter from modernity is inserted into the Christian story, or when a postmodern character is reborn into the epic of restoration. Such chapters must be carefully rewritten to comport with the biblical metanarrative; and such characters must be transformed in order to play their new role faithfully.

Hearing and Telling the Story

Currently, I am rereading the Old Testament. I'm allowing the stories (and songs!) to shape who I am and how I view the world. Tony Campolo and William Willimon suggest, "In reading the Bible we are asked to relinquish the tight grip of the world's officially approved stories in order to be embraced solely by God's story. The Bible is better than a book of rules. It is a way of transferring us into a new world, of bringing us, step by step, closer to the Kingdom of God." Certainly I believe the stories to be true. I trust that the events actually happened. But my eyes have been opened and my imagination liberated by the freedom of simply allowing the story to shape who I am. I hope the same is happening for the men in my Bible study at the rehab center—and for you.

Have you ever gotten totally lost in a story? I don't mean that you couldn't figure out what was going on. I mean have you ever lost *yourself* in the story? You know, you go to a great movie, and you totally lose track of time. Upon leaving the theater you have to remind yourself what day it is, what time it is, where you are. Or you are reading a great novel, and the next thing you know it's 3:00 a.m. and you've got to be up at 7:00. Sometimes it feels really good to get lost in a story. I imagine that wanna-be lovers are most easily entranced by romances, and wanna-be heroes fall prey to good action dramas. I suppose I had something like that in mind when I wrote this little poem a few months back—with one key difference: I don't want to be mesmerized by a powerful movie. I want to be part of some drama myself, a grand epic in which actors play important roles.

ONE DAY

Today spins like so many lost days,
the celluloid serpent looped in the projector.
I watch, slouch and slide into the story,
cast images on the wall.

Upon waking, before fear takes form, dreams
   flicker.
Blink. Alpha waves of memory, good sweat beads.
Blink, blink . . . Men rut, and women, all together,
sad slots, parallel story lines never crossed.

On screen parade best boys, body doubles, key grips,
in a hurry;
without pausing previews of the next story—*please
make it good!*
Not another Omega Doom, apocalyptic memo
that all stories end.

Each story thin as film,
vicarious victory *du jour.*
I want to be the hero once—
staring down demons, saving civilization,
standing, turning, and going out.

I share this poem because I know that you feel the same thing that I do. You too want to rise above the flicker of images to find yourself in a real story of consequence and to live a life that matters. God has invited you into just such a story. Good storytellers invite outsiders to live in their story. Once inside a story, new listeners may decide that the story "rings true." They hear the story as their own. The biblical story has appeal because it is so comprehensive and coherent, so true to cosmic order and human experience. Once people listen intently and enter the story, many are hooked. In the final analysis, however, the story isn't embraced simply due to its merits. The embrace of God brings people into the story.

We don't really need to imagine our way into a story world. Our world, even our academic world, is already storied. College curricula are rather like scripts or stage directions for a story. In its curricula, a college organizes disciplines and texts and requirements to introduce students to something (the liberal arts, job readiness, critical thinking, responsible citizenship). As students take various courses, they are being socialized to live in a story, or perhaps they encounter numerous unrelated stories. In commentary on Dante's *Inferno* T. S. Eliot writes, "Hell is the place where nothing connects to nothing." I sometimes grieve for college students because I believe that there is more than a little hell in what most are experiencing. Nothing connects. A good curriculum (and co-curriculum) should help lead students to develop wisdom and discernment, to live a life of humility and curiosity and delight. A good curriculum tells a story and invites students to participate in that story. Don't expect to find that story clearly articulated in the curriculum or co-curriculum of your school, even if you are attending a Christian institution. No matter where you are, you will need to learn how to live out the biblical story while you are simultaneously being tugged by other tales.

There is good news. One day there will be a place, not *where nothing connects to nothing,* but where everything connects to the One and is framed by the story of the Three. That story is afoot.

Discussion Questions

1. If you were to write the story of your life (an autobiography), what would the title be? Try to sketch an outline of your story. What are some of twists and turns? Are there any villains or heroes? Would you say that your story has been shaped by the biblical story or by another life-shaping story?
2. Jesus was a story teller. He often told stories, or parables, as an invitation for the hearer to enter into a story and find the theological meaning by becoming one of the characters. For example, read Luke 10:25–37 and Matthew 25:14–30. Why do you think

Jesus taught in this way? What do you learn from these stories? What other parables come to mind?

3. Have you ever gotten totally lost in a story? Describe the experience.
4. Is the academy part of a story, and should it be part of the Christian story?
5. T. S. Eliot wrote, "Hell is the place where nothing connects to nothing." Have you experienced college as a fragmented piece of "hell," or have you experienced educational gestalt?

Recommendations

Lesslie Newbigin, *A Walk Through the Bible* (Vancouver, BC: Regent College Publishing, 2005).

Craig G. Bartholomew and Michael W. Goheen, *The Drama of Scripture: Finding Our Place in the Biblical Story* (Grand Rapids: Baker Academic, 2004).

FISH-EYED LEARNING

CHAPTER 5

I 've caught a few walleye in my day. I guess they get that name because, like most fish, it doesn't look like they should be able to see what's right in front of their noses. I'd be wall-eyed (well, technically it would be *divergent strabismus*) if I could stick my head between two books and dedicate an eye to each. This might cut my study time in half, but it might cut my social life in half as well.

Fish-eye means something completely different to a photographer. A fish-eye lens helps a photographer capture a 180-degree panoramic view. In this chapter we want to provide a kind of panorama of Christian learning. To do this we will simply apply the contours of the biblical story to the challenge that is before us—academic faithfulness. Before we get to that, let me say a brief word about a monster and his brain.

The Disembodied Mind

In *Young Frankenstein*, Mel Brooks's comedy movie version of Mary Shelley's classic, *Frankenstein,* things start to go terribly wrong when the hunch-backed lab assistant Igor retrieves the wrong brain for the monster's transplant surgery. Instead of coming back with Einstein's brain, he comes back with the brain of Abby Normal. It's bad enough that the monster has to put up with an oversized, rough-stitched corpse for a body. Now he's gotta put up with a rotten brain as well.

Apparently many people feel that Christians, at least those labeled evangelicals, have got rotten brains too. Even "insiders"—Christian scholars like Os Guinness, Mark Noll, and George Marsden—have described the evangelical mind as flabby, scandalous, and outrageous. This makes the Christian mind sound like a lazy, blubbery brain, just sitting there and in great need of exercise. Yet these scholars do not disparage the possibility of the Christian mind, only that such a mind has not been a deep concern of evangelical Christianity. We'd like to see that change. We'd like to start a fitness campaign for the Christian mind. That is why we want to recruit you to become a deeply thoughtful Christian, exercising your brain to get it in shape for service. You do this not just by becoming a Bible scholar (although we surely need to study the scriptures seriously), but by bringing Christian conviction to bear on the whole of the collegiate experience.

What is this Christian mind? Or asked in slightly different ways—

- Is there something distinctive about a Christian point of view?
- Are there explicitly Christian contours of thinking and Christian purposes of knowing?
- In what ways do Christians *think* differently, or *see* things differently?
- Is there a uniquely Christian perspective of my major or academic discipline?

The Bible is clear that the mind matters and that we are called to develop certain patterns and priorities in our thinking. Each of us is responsible to "renew our minds" (Romans 12:2), to "take every thought captive" (2 Corinthians 10:5), to do everything "in the name of the Lord Jesus" (Colossians 3:17), and to "seek first his kingdom" (Matt. 6:33). A thorough theology of the Christian mind or a Christian perspective on academics would not only interrogate these texts in some depth, but it would also explore pervasive biblical themes of wisdom, stewardship, and discipleship. In such a theology we would discover that *knowing* and the *Christian mind* are not divorced from other aspects of Christian faithfulness. The fullness of knowing includes the "doing" response. In other words, the Christian mind is connected to Christian character and Christian action. This more thorough-going theology might also reveal to us the close connections between knowing and loving. We are, after all, to love the Lord our God with all our minds.

> Love the Lord your God with all your heart and with all your soul and with all your mind and with all your strength. (Mark 12:30)

The Christian mind is not an independent entity; it is not a disembodied mind. It is a mind that is always in relationship and a mind that is being shaped in those relationships. *In Christ is hidden all the treasures of wisdom and knowledge* (Colossians 2:3). Christians have been purchased by Christ's sacrifice and reconciled to God through him. The Holy Spirit is active in the life of the believer. Here we have not only the foundations for a philosophy of knowing, but a reminder that the Christian mind is fundamentally relational. Understanding who we are and what we are supposed to be doing will require us to attend to our relationship with God. The Christian mind is developed in relationship with God, who has revealed himself in creation, by scriptural revelation, in the living word, Jesus, and by his Holy Spirit.

Much more can be said (and needs to be said) about creational revelation as well as about the dynamics of God's revelation to us through the persons of the Trinity. But for now, let's just focus on this one piece—how does the Bible shape the Christian mind? Certainly the Bible reveals the Christ by whom this fundamental relationship to God is even possible. Our Christian academic work has Jesus Christ at the start, at the center, at the end. He is the Alpha and Omega of our thinking. Is there more?

Thinking Scripturally

Christian thinking is biblically patterned. The contours of this Christian story shape the contours of the Christian mind. In other words, the Christian story ought to become so much our own that we can't help but think in terms of its major themes. As we discussed in chapter three, the biblical story is sometimes outlined as Creation, Fall, Redemption, and Consummation. This approach takes the whole testimony of God into account as the unfolding story of God's redemptive purposes, administered by God's own faithful initiatives and promises, his covenant, and achieved through the gospel of Jesus Christ. This chapter is designed to help you begin to put the biblical story to work. It isn't enough to *know* the story. We've got to begin to live in it and to see everything else through it.

Creation

Fundamental assumptions about the nature of reality lie behind every academic theory and every discipline. The assumption that the physical world is all that there is, for example, will shape not only one's approach to the natural sciences but to the social sciences, humanities, arts, and professions as well. On the other hand, academic work based on a biblical theology of creation will be distinctive in important ways. The Christian scholar and student views God as the creator of all things, the One who designed the creation for human flourishing and development. The Christian scholar and student will expect and discover order, marvel at intricacies and mysteries, and seek to unlock the goodness and potential that God has placed in his very good creation. She will honor God through her research and writing, and she will contest the ideas and practices that despoil the creation, deform culture, and harm human beings made in God's image. Her work in the academy is to faithfully interpret, steward, and cultivate our God-made home. Anything she studies—from cellular biology, to the complexities of adolescent psychology, to the history of political thought, to civil engineering—will be seen as a chance to explore creational realities. Every *thing* is part of God's creation, and academic disciplines should be developed, not to exploit the things of creation, but to understand them faithfully.

Fall

Humanity's fall into sin as described in Genesis 3 is a foundational story for biblical people. The perverse and pervasive implications of the fall shadow the entire history of the human race. Sin is more than the misdeeds individuals do and more than good deeds left undone. Sin corrupts not only the will but the mind as well. In fact, sin has taken root at the very heart of every human being, and this weed must be pulled out, every bit of it. Sin doesn't simply reside within us; it takes root in social practices, institutional policies, cultural values, and in everything that is overgrown by human pride and contempt for the Creator. Due to sin, the good but marred creation is under God's curse and judgment, and it is despoiled (although not completely ruined) by the Evil One, the parasite and perverter of the good things of God's creation.

The effects of the fall reach into every aspect of creation, and consequently into every discipline. Christian students ask: What are the lies or ideological confusions that distort my discipline and my approach to this discipline? One part of every Christian's work, including academic work, is confession of sin. Together we should confess that wisdom and compassion and justice and integrity are often absent from our work—in the lab, in the classroom, and in our own thinking. We won't get it right right away, and we'll never get it altogether right.

It takes time to develop a Christian perspective, and a lifetime to contend with the ravages of sin. We contend with sin, not just in our own personal lives but also in our intellectual lives. Confronting unbiblical ideologies and theories that have distorted the various fields of study in God's world is part of our academic task.

Redemption

Enumerating the glories of the gospel of Jesus Christ would take us well beyond the scope of this chapter. This gospel is the source of redemption and power. Without Jesus the whole world would remain in the clutches of the enemy and each of us would remain powerless to mount resistance. The work of Christ is not limited to the redemption of individuals. Christ died for the entire creation (Colossians 1:20; Ephesians 1:7–10). His resurrection is good news for every aspect of the creation (Romans 8:22–23). Those who are redeemed in Christ are also called in him to engage in the reconciliation and restoration that mark the ongoing work of Christ in his creation (Luke 4:14–21, 2 Corinthians 5:17–20). What is the good that God had in mind? Institutions and theories, hobbies and jobs, organizational systems and ecosystems—all may honor God, and all require the care of good stewards to do so.

As Christian students we should seek to comprehend the good of God-made structures, counter the lies and heal the scars of sin, and contribute to the development of neighbor-loving relationships and God-honoring cultural development. The biblical gospel is the good news of individual salvation, but it is also the good news of the kingdom, the healing and restoration of the creation itself. Jesus himself is constantly referring to his work as the gospel of the kingdom. He offers not only forgiveness but also healing and guidance toward a new way of being human in the world. Jesus cares about healing his diseased creation. He is the good physician, and we are the orderlies instructed to attend to the healing process.

Consummation

Faithful students are pulled on by the hope of the coming kingdom. They are guided in their own daily efforts by the knowledge that the justice and peace of God has come in Christ and will burst into spectacular beauty in the final consummation when Jesus actually returns to earth. This is not to suggest that we are on an easy progressive march toward realizing the kingdom of God on earth. That would give too much credit to our ability and too little to the depth and tenacity of sin in the world. One day Christ will return, and in that day of judgment sin will be eradicated and the new heavens and new earth will be ushered in by the Judge and King!

> Then I saw a new heaven and a new earth, for the first heaven and the first earth had passed away, and there was no longer any sea. I saw the Holy City, the new Jerusalem, coming down out of heaven from God, prepared as a bride beautifully dressed for her husband. And I heard a loud voice from the throne saying, "Now the dwelling of God is with men, and he will live with them. They will be his people, and God himself will be with them and be their God. He will wipe every tear from their eyes. There will be no more death or mourning or crying or pain, for the old order of things has passed away." He who was seated on the throne said, "I am making everything new!" Then he said, "Write this down, for these words are trustworthy and true." (Revelation 21:1–5)

> Then the angel showed me the river of the water of life, as clear as crystal, flowing from the throne of God and of the Lamb down the middle of the great street of the city. On each side of the river stood the tree of life, bearing twelve crops of fruit, yielding its fruit every month. And the leaves of the tree are for the healing of the nations. No longer will there be any curse. The throne of God and of the Lamb will be in the city, and his servants will serve him. They will see his face, and his name will be on their foreheads. There will be no more night. They will not need the light of a lamp or the light of the sun, for the Lord God will give them light. And they will reign for ever and ever. (Revelation 22:1–5)

While we await the day of reckoning and restoration, we do not wait sitting on our hands, squandering our talents, and silencing our minds. Instead, we live each day enjoying the blessings of the gospel and pursuing the hope that has been revealed. We live to see the international reach of the gospel, to imagine local economic development programs, to protect biodiversity from environmental contamination, to nurture loving families and churches, and to enjoy the arts in full bloom of color and sound and movement. While these cultural fruits may not exactly be the kingdom, they are certainly harbingers of the now and future reign of God. Such work posts the world with signs—*Hope Alive!* and *Kingdom Coming!*

In this chapter we have reviewed some biblical texts and theological concepts. We aren't suggesting that every faithful student needs to become a Bible major. We are suggesting, however, that without insight into the major themes of the scripture it will be impossible to develop a Christian mind. Good churches and campus fellowship groups attend to this through biblical preaching and rigorous Christian education. You can begin now to exercise your Christian mind by getting involved in a Bible study and by reading a few books that will help you develop a Christian perspective. One eye in the Word and the other on the matter at hand. This won't make you cross-eyed—in fact, you will begin to see more clearly than ever before.

Discussion Questions

1. Have you encountered the notion of a "Christian mind"?
2. What keeps us from developing our minds and loving God with our minds?
3. Fundamental assumptions about the nature of reality lie behind every academic theory and every disci-

pline. How have you noticed this? Why is recognizing fundamental assumptions crucial to academic faithfulness?

4. Have you recognized the "lies or ideological confusions" in your discipline or in any of your courses?

5. Read Acts 17:16–34. Does this story suggest implications for academic faithfulness?

Recommendations

Clifford Williams, *Life of the Mind: A Christian Perspective* (Grand Rapids: Baker Academic, 2002).

Harry Blamires, *A Christian Mind: How Should a Christian Think?* (Vancouver, BC: Regent College Publishing, 2005).

James Emery White, *A Mind For God* (Downers Grove, IL: InterVarsity Press, 2006).

FOUR-I-ED LEARNING

CHAPTER 6

We should not feel too tightly constrained by the theological terms of the previous chapter (creation, fall, redemption, and consummation). In fact, other words are often used that carry similar freight. In the four brief sections that follow, we've arranged reflections on four other words that are useful for the student pursuing academic faithfulness. Each of these words illustrates, in a slightly different way, the main sections of the biblical drama. While creation-fall-redemption-consummation outlines the biblical story, integration-idolatry-investment-imagination (we hope) will help you forge a clearer connection to faithful learning. These four i's should help you see what learning is really about.

Four-i-ed Learning

integration ↔ creation
idolatry ↔ fall
investment ↔ redemption
imagination ↔ consummation

Integration

The word *integrate* means to bring things together, to unify them somehow. The goal is *integrity*—a seamless whole. When we say that a person has integrity, generally what we mean is that they are not two-faced or double minded. They do not display a Jekyll and Hyde personality, but rather they are honest, straightforward, and sincere. The word *integration* has been used in Christian circles to mark the crucial intersection, or more accurately, to highlight the deep, rich, and essential connections between faith and learning. While integration isn't a biblical word, it is a biblical idea. The Bible has a great deal to say about faithful allegiance to God, who is the Three in One. Unity is seen as ultimate even where the Bible touches on the mystery of the Trinity. And even in the midst of the many things of God's creation, faithfulness is all about remembering the One, and acknowledging that *the many* comes from the One.

Christians have a distinct advantage over others seeking to develop an integrated perspective. We know the source of integration. God alone is the One, and he alone is the fountain of meaning. Integration is linked to the biblical idea of creation. God is the source of both the diversity of the creation and of the unity that makes sense of the creation. Everything else in the creation is not the One, and nothing in the creation can function as an ultimate anchor for the things in the creation. We try to understand things in connection to their Creator, and consequently we try to comprehend how various aspects of life in the world ought to honor God and ought to connect with each other to bring about the creational harmony and peace (shalom) desired by God. Seeking the wisdom and insight that connects our beliefs about God who is One, and the things of the creation (every academic discipline, every activity, every institution) has been labeled "the integration of faith and learning."

Another phrase made popular by Arthur Holmes captures this well: *All truth is God's truth.* In a brief book about a Christian agenda for higher education, Holmes described integration in a helpful way. Holmes is a sharp thinker who has been pondering this topic for a long time. Here he is addressing Christian institutions, but the same concerns apply to Christians wherever they are studying.

> [A distinctive approach to Christian higher education] should be an education that cultivates the creative and active integration of faith and learning, of faith and culture . . . it must under no circumstance become a disjunction between piety and scholarship, faith and reason, religion and science. . . . Integration also transcends awkward conjunctions of faith and learning in some unholy alliance rather than a fruitful union. What we need is not Christians who are also scholars but Christian scholars, not Christianity alongside education but Christian education. It shuns tacked-on moralizing and applications. . . . It requires a thorough analysis of methods and materials and concepts and theoretical structures, a lively and rigorous interpenetration of liberal learning with the content and commitment of Christian faith.

The notion of integration of faith and learning has become a cliché at some Christian colleges. Perhaps this is because it is not a simple method or something that can be accomplished in four years. Integration is a constant challenge to those seeking to be authentic Christian students and scholars. We must continually seek to integrate our beliefs with the testimony of scripture, our words with our beliefs, our actions with our words, and our academic work with our theology. Pursuing integrity (faithfulness) in these areas is a key aspect of our shared calling. In other words, the task of Christian students is lifelong and daily faithfulness to the One. This faithfulness calls us together to discern what God has revealed regarding our place and responsibility in his world—as artists and athletes, citizens and consumers, employees and employers, students and teachers.

Arthur Holmes is also instructive regarding a different aspect of integration: interdisciplinary learning. In Holmes's view, an interdisciplinary approach to learning is critical because it is the natural pedagogical byproduct of a commitment to holistic learning. According to Holmes, holistic learning helps students to "see things in relationship, to organize ideas into an ordered whole, to be systematic, to work toward a unified understanding." (Remember gestalt?)

Richard Slimbach challenges teachers to push toward a rich and penetrating interdisciplinary approach. Even if some of your college profs don't take his advice, we think you should approach your education in this manner:

> [I]n addressing the issue of globalization, no single discipline will enable students to see the relationships between deforestation and shopping malls, free trade and urban migration, new technologies and street crime, international aid and increased hunger. They are too readily handled as random, disconnected facts and not as threads of a single cloth. Educating students to *think interdisciplinary* means that merely acquainting students with a variety of disciplinary offerings (as is done in the typical general education program) is insufficient. Our central concern should be to help students *unify* their fragments of knowledge into a cohesive, meaningful, and missional vision for life. But this assumes that we, as educators, see that vision clearly ourselves.

The integration of faith and learning and interdisciplinary integration do not go far enough in describing faithful learning. Comprehending coherence and recognizing our dependence on God is part of academic faithfulness, but we also must recognize that the Bible portrays a seamless continuity between our *knowing* and our *doing*. Having an integrated perspective is not the goal; an integrated life is the goal. Learning isn't merely for job readiness or self-advancement. Learning ought to be a way to love God and neighbor, a way to care for the creation and develop healthy communities.

When I think back about the college learning experiences that really hit me hard and continue to shape me now, almost all of them were experiences that led me to discover integration in some way or another. I came to see the relevance of my faith while addressing a social or scientific problem. I still remember discovering the benefit of a multidisciplinary approach for understanding addictive behavior, and this insight came through discussions with addicts. On another occasion I really learned about homelessness by doing something about it. Real learning is thick, and it is for life. It is not sterile, fragmented, and boring, though "school" sometimes is.

Idolatry

The natural harmony and integration of God's good creation was lost when the world was subjected to sin and chaos through human disobedience. In the new culture and new history that began east of Eden, human beings began to live according to their own agenda. They turned from the One and began to worship idols of their own construction. They developed cultures that aggrandized their own accomplishments. God warned again and again that idols, imposters to be sure, delivered death to those who followed them (Exodus 20:1–6). Idols are always hungry, and they devour those who worship them (Psalm 115). As we read the ancient histories of Israel, identifying idols is not so tricky—the golden calf, Baal, Asherah, and Dagon are all sculpted gods. We learn in the New Testament accounts that idols are nothing in themselves (1 Corinthians 8:4), yet they do represent flagrant unfaithfulness. Paul even identifies immaterial unfaithfulness, like greed, as idolatry (Ephesians 5:5; Colossians 3:5). Such gods are tougher to identify than the sculpted gods of ancient Israel.

In our own day, we must continue in the prophetic work of flagging dangerous idols. Posting signs on dangerous roads or at the edge of a cliff is a way of caring for others. Posting warnings on bad ideas is likewise a very important way to care not just about "the truth" but actually to care for others who might fall to the lies. Perhaps we shouldn't mimic Isaiah's tone in Isaiah 44 where he ridicules the idol, its maker, and those duped into the worship of a wooden totem. But we do perform a great service to church and society—and the colleges where we find ourselves—when we unmask idols.

Idols love to find their way into educational institutions, textbooks, and theories. From there they gain adherents and draw the unsuspecting into lives of bondage. Most college students, even many beloved professors, do not view academics this way. They think of academic work as neutral, and they view faith as irrelevant to the task. Our culture is so disinterested in radical loyalty to God that we don't recognize idolatrous ideologies, unbiblical worldviews, and incoherent value systems. But the Bible is clear that our task is to "demolish arguments and every pretension that sets itself up against the knowledge of God" (2 Corinthians 10:5). Even when we feel powerless to demolish the idols of our day, we still post our warnings and pray for the rescue of the One who is in no way powerless for such destruction.

A Christian perspective is fundamentally different from every perspective that is not Christian. This is sometimes called the *antithesis*. Jesus Christ is Lord of all, contending for his own creation against every false claim upon it and every false lord that claims it. Light has come into the darkness; the kingdom of God has been planted in the midst of the kingdoms of this world. As we discussed in the previous chapter, Christians should not fall sway to either the spirit of modernity or postmodernity, for neither are ultimately expressions of the spirit of God. In both modernity and postmodernity life in the world is shaped not by the biblical story, but by a story of human construction. A Christian perspective will contend with both, for both arise from a spirit of human control and autonomy. A Christian perspective is grounded in the Christian story and ultimately in Jesus Christ himself. No other aspect of creation can be the ultimate point of reference. That is how idols are born.

Idols wear many disguises, and they go incognito to fit into particular disciplines. A critique of economic ideologies, for example, should emerge as Christian students and open-minded professors and godly scholars and faithful business people seek to build on Christian principles such as stewardship. Deep Christian thinking will generally lead one not to embrace existing options. In other words, Christian economic theory will likely be neither socialist nor capitalist, but some kind of alternative approach will emerge. This quest for biblically grounded theory or faithful models for Christian living is sometimes referred to as the "third way." Third-way thinking about economics will likely include deep concerns regarding social justice, the needs of the poor, overconsumption, and the danger of the consolidation of wealth in the hands of too few (sounds a little left, eh?). But faithful thinking about economics will also be realistic about job formation, the comparative success of open markets, and the limits of governmental control (sounds a little right, eh?).

This is not to say that a Christian view always finds its place in the middle. Sometimes a Christian perspective may lead us to embrace a very conservative position or policy, and at other times we may need to paint our signs and prepare to march. Idols surround us, and perhaps they inhabit perspectives that we already hold dear. Identifying idols is difficult academic work and requires discernment, prayer, and ongoing dialogue. Identifying the idols is just the start. Developing uniquely Christian points of view on important topics requires serious study, wide dialogue, and a great deal of courage.

God pours out good gifts and wisdom on believers and unbelievers alike. Sometimes this is called *common grace*. Christians have much to learn from those who do not share their perspective. Great literature may be written by arrogant atheists, and, conversely, good theologians may make very bad scientists. We must learn to acknowledge good insights wherever they arise and to reappropriate those insights into a faithfully integrated worldview. This is not unlike what Paul did on Mars Hill (Acts 17), when he cited popular pagan poetry to build a bridge with his very academic and rather hostile listeners.

Most of the textbooks that we read in college are not written by Christian authors. This is inevitable, and it can be exceedingly helpful to students as long as they are trained to discern the distortions and limitations of alternative perspectives. Students must be on guard, as we have said, but they can also relax in the knowledge that "all truth is God's truth." Most college professors, even those who have studied under idolatrous ideologies and are perplexed by the notion of an integrated worldview, love their disciplines and care for their students. Thanks to God's common grace, we can honor the efforts of good professors as they seek to grasp and teach truth.

Investment

We are still in the middle of this argument—that having a good grasp on a biblical worldview and Christian theology is essential in order for a Christian mind to develop. There is certainly disagreement on what the most essential ingredients of such a theology really are. Different Christian traditions place emphasis on different aspects of the Bible. In some traditions, for example, the gospel is viewed primarily as rescue from sin and the promise of heaven. While this view emphasizes the urgent call to evangelism, it offers little to help shape a theology of culture or an ethic for life in the world, especially the academic world. In other traditions, the gospel is seen not only as rescue but also as restoration—the restoration of human beings to become again what they were created to be, and the restoration of the whole creation to become again what God created it to be. In this view all of life falls under the lordship of Christ. Faithfulness is to be expressed in every field and endeavor. Our work in this life is not for bread alone. Our sweaty labor is lifted and offered as a sacrifice of praise in hopes that it will one day be purified (1 Corinthians 3:10). This is what the faithful follower of Jesus Christ wants to hear: "Well done, good and faithful servant" (Matthew

25:23). This perspective provides assurance that we can find meaning in our studies and in our work.

All kinds of work can be done to the glory of God (Colossians 3:17). No reasonable work done for the Lord should be disparaged. Certainly, many people need to engage in work as a means to provide food for family, but the Christian call is deeper still. Christians ought to pursue work that displays neighbor-love and contributes to the common good. We need to study and work, not for success, but instead as an expression of faithfulness and service. A bookshelf five feet long at my local Barnes and Noble store holds books that have been written to help people "find meaning in their work" or to inject "spirit in the workplace." Apparently this is a great concern, and it is understandable. Who wants to spend forty or sixty hours each week doing something that feels meaningless? Even if it pays well, that still isn't much consolation. A view of life and work shaped by the Bible is the best response to the crisis of empty work. We need to revive a spirituality of work in our day, a Christianity that is alive from 9 to 5 (and beyond)! Of course, we also need to learn the limits of work and the joy of deep investment in other areas of life as well: families, communities, the environment, the arts, and playfulness to name a few.

Once a Christian comes to believe that life matters, that the creation is designed for the flourishing of life, and that God cares about life in this world, then our investment in work and all kinds of things takes on a new significance. Relationships matter, and even broken ones can be reconciled. Communities matter and can be restored. Every school needs good teachers who know and love God, who care for students, and who are prepared to develop curricula that invite students into learning that really matters. Businesses need faithful accountants and creative (not manipulative) marketing agents. Our churches need good pastors and leaders, and lay people need to be encouraged not only to invest themselves in their local church but also to consider God's interests in the work that they do. Without significant investment, without an ethic for life in the world, work becomes soulless, communities wither, churches empty, relationships erode, and we grow bored and frustrated.

Imagination

Our world needs to hear the voices of articulate, modern-day prophets (like you?) who measure *what is* against *what should be*. We've already talked a good bit about *what is* (the creation, in which everything is twisted by sin). How do we begin to envision *what should be*? As we discussed in the previous section, Christians are encouraged to invest in the restoration of the creation. They are to embody the concerns of God in his own world. And yet we also know that, in the end, it is not human effort that ushers in the final consummation, that future time when all things are made new. Christians are enjoined to be prepared and to await the day with eager anticipation. It seems strange to *eagerly await* a cataclysmic transformation. But it feels less strange to those burdened with the sorrow and pains of this broken age. And it feels less strange to those that begin to imagine—to ponder, reflect upon, anticipate—the glories of the age to come.

We catch but a glimpse of this hope in Revelation 21–22 (we saw portions of this text in the previous chapter). Here we see Eden in full bloom, stretched big as a city. God once again dwells with his people. He wipes away every sorrow, heals every hurt, illuminates every dark place. Peace is the rule of every day, love is the bond between all people, and beauty beams even from the foundation stones. Perhaps this state of affairs is best described by the Hebrew word *shalom*. This word for peace is a "dwelling" word. It is expressed well in the Old Testament visions of the prophets, who described a coming restoration in which deserts would bloom into new life, lions would sleep peacefully next to lambs, the implements of war would be reshaped as plows, and all people would live in harmony. This is a picture of the healing of creation. Shalom is the peace of God dwelling with us, and of human community dwelling together in the blessing that comes with God's nearness. In shalom, perhaps it will be difficult to stop singing, or to stop laughing, or to stop leaping.

In the meantime, we enjoy morsels of joy and peace. And part of our work is to serve them about—like hors d'oeuvres before the banquet. Even our academic work must be punctuated with celebration and stretched by anticipation. We are, after all, to practice what will be in a world that is not yet.

With shalom in view, imagining becomes a significant aspect of our learning. Our imaginations need to be liberated from status quo aspirations and dreams of self-fulfillment. We need to look beyond *the way things are* toward *the way things may be*. Our renewed imaginations need to be joined with hoping, and our hopes worded in prayer, and our prayers need to rise up into commitments that pump compassion and courage into our lives. Richard Middleton and Brian Walsh suggest several questions to help ignite biblical imagination:

> A liberated imagination is a prerequisite for facing the future. Consequently, we need to ask ourselves some honest questions. Can we *imagine* a politics of justice and compassion in place of the present global politics of

oppression and economic idolatry? Dare we *imagine* an economics of equality and care in place of the dominant economics of affluence and poverty? Can we *imagine* our work life to be at one with our worship—an act of service and praise, rather than a grim necessity or a means to an affluent lifestyle? Can we *imagine* a society which has broken through its morbid preoccupation with death and instead truly affirms life, both at the fetal stage and in all of its dimensions? Is a relationship of friendship, instead of exploitation, with the rest of the creation *imaginable?* Is it *imaginable* that the mass media could be an agent of awakened social, cultural and spiritual renewal, rather than the one thing that most numbs us into cultural complacency and sleep? And is our imagination open enough to conceive of a business enterprise that is characterized by stewardship, environmental responsibility and real serviceability, rather than profits, pollution, and the production and marketing of superfluous consumer goods? If we cannot have such a liberated imagination and cannot countenance such radical dreams, then the story remains closed for us and we have no hope.

Unfortunately, imagination is not a central concern of the academy, and our own culture anesthetizes our creativity. We rely on the imaginations of professionals—you know, the ones who make the fabulous movies, the addictive games, the ubiquitous ads. We are taught to imagine in pop-culture terms and to purchase en masse. In a context like this, developing a biblical imagination won't be easy. I imagine that it will take shape as we imitate the prophets. They were used by God because of their growing dis-ease with the way things were and their hopeful imagination of what one day would come. Can you imagine how God might want things to change in your family, or at school, or church, or workplace? Is it *imaginable* that the spirit is calling us to "go deeper," to think outside of the box, and to creatively and collaboratively engage in the ongoing restoration of God's world?

We hope that the four-i-ed approach to faithful learning discussed in this chapter will help you make connections, discern lies, and live with purpose, a purpose that is connected to the purposes of God. The starting point is crucial, and perhaps we haven't spent enough time there. Are you sold out to following Christ alone as Lord? Do you sense that he really does care about your academic work? Are you willing to struggle with the implications of a Christian worldview in your classwork, labs, academic habits, and future investments? We believe that the Spirit is calling this generation of Christian collegians to go deeper. Can you imagine yourself being a part of it all?

Herbie's Bible

Herbie is beginning to get the picture. I've tightened my interview with him up a little, but it captures accurately Herbie's discovery.

> ***Herbie, what do you understand the Bible to be about?***
> I always thought the Bible was a collection of prohibitions and laws. I knew that Jesus came into view toward the end and that the Bible contained an offer of forgiveness and salvation. And I've believed the gospel for five or six years now. But it wasn't until this year that I came to see that the Bible is much more than teachings about morality and salvation. It is an invitation into something big—you know, the kingdom. And the invitation is to get involved, to begin to take up God's concerns, and to live with joy and purpose in God's world.

How do you read the Bible?

For a while I was trying to read the Bible every day, about a chapter a day. That was good. What helped most was getting together to talk over the things I read with a group of friends. These conversations have become a kind of Bible study. We read a short book of the Bible or some parable or something, and then we get together to talk about it. . . . I used to read the Bible to make me feel better, or to find the answer to some question that I had. Now I'm a little more patient with the Bible, and I don't always expect it to be about me. I've come to see God more in the story, to understand what he is up to and what he cares about.

How do you connect the Bible to your work in the classroom?

I had a religion class first semester, and we touched on the Bible and other sacred writings. The Bible hasn't been either required or suggested reading in any of my other classes. But I know that somehow I've got to connect what I'm reading in the Bible to what I'm learning in my classes. Now that I am beginning to understand the Christian faith a little better, I recognize that I'm learning things in classes that don't fit with what I'm reading in the Bible. So I guess I'm trying to learn how to be critical, in a good way, about my textbooks and about what my professors say. I suppose I could be doing more to figure this out, but I'm not sure what to do.

What launched you on this journey of academic faithfulness?

At first it was one passage that haunted me. I kept on thinking about it and wondering what it meant for me. I came across it in 2 Corinthians, where Paul is addressing the leaders of the church in Corinth. And this is a city full of problems, and evidently the devil-may-care attitude of the city had saturated the church as well. Paul was trying to rattle the status quo, almost like he was a coach trying to psych a team up for a big game. But the battle he envisioned wasn't a big game, it was about life, and in a way, about academic life.

We demolish arguments and every pretension that sets itself up against the knowledge of God, and we take captive every thought to make it obedient to Christ. (2 Corinthians 10:5)

That passage really got me thinking. What are the arguments and pretensions that are deluding me? What might it mean to take every thought captive to Christ? That verse got under my skin for about a month or so before I found a small group of other students who were willing to discuss these questions. And that is where it all began.

Herbie is a wise young man. He is studying the Bible, discussing it with friends, and at least trying to connect it to his work in the classroom. There is more he could do, and we'll discuss some ideas, but he is off to a good start. I didn't get to this point until my junior year. Herbie was a freshman last year. He was trying to develop good habits for his time in college. Kudos to the man.

Discussion Questions

1. This chapter includes vocabulary that may be new to you. We think these words are important. Define the following terms and explain how they were used in this chapter:

   Integration
   Idolatry
   Shalom

Antithesis
Third-way
Common grace

2. What does it look like to integrate faith and learning? Why is simply having an integrated "perspective" not the goal?
3. Why is imagination so important to academic faithfulness?
4. Do you read the Bible the way Herbie does?

Recommendations

Cornelius Plantinga Jr., *Engaging God's World: A Christian Vision of Faith, Learning, and Living* (Grand Rapids: Eerdmans, 2002).

Steven Garber, *The Fabric of Faithfulness: Weaving Together Belief and Behavior*, 2nd ed. (Downers Grove, IL: InterVarsity Press, 2007).

EMBODYING THE OUTRAGEOUS IDEA

CHAPTER 7

My first two-wheeler came from a junkyard. It was spray-painted royal blue, was missing both fenders, and had a plastic seat contoured to fit a small child. The seat worked out fine because I was a small child. My bike had no training wheels, and over the years I've forgotten most of the crashes and skinned knees, so I can say now with cruel certainty that every child should learn to ride without the aid of pathetic pamper wheels. My mom or dad or sister would run alongside me and my bike and launch us down the sidewalk. I'd glide for a second or two. Sadly, I was a very slow learner, but happily, a quick healer. And then one day when my sister launched me down the sidewalk, I was steady somehow, peddling, soaring. I felt like I was riding my bike into the sky. I still remember shouting to my Mom and Dad who were raking leaves in the yard. They waved wildly, and I waved back. Unfortunately, I hadn't yet mastered the riding wave.

If my blue bike had come with a manual, I would have thrown it right in the trash—I was, after all, a small boy. But even today I still discard manuals for most things. Some things certainly require detailed instructions. Other things you learn best simply by doing them, like golf. I've watched too many golf videos, and I've read *Golf Digest* religiously for several years. Yet on most days I am still the most dangerous golfer on the course. I've always been jealous of a friend of mine, Bob, who is easily the best athlete I have ever known. He watched a half-hour of a golf tournament on TV one day and later that day displayed a perfect golf swing. He beat me by ten strokes his first time on a golf course. Bob's mind and body are seamlessly connected. If he can picture it, he can do it. I remember a time when Bob watched some MTV music videos and later that evening was the life of the party, imitating Madonna and several other trashy dancers. Bob isn't just a kinesthetic learner, he is a kinesthetic genius. We can all learn by watching and doing; it's just that most of us aren't perfectly attuned to our bodies. Even those of us who like to learn by reading benefit from putting our bodies into motion.

Over the summer, our college student Bible study group had been reading and discussing a rather difficult book of the Bible. At one of our meetings toward the end of our study, Michael asked, "Should I be changing in any way as a result of this study? I understand that perhaps I should be thinking differently about certain things, but how should I actually be changing? What should I *do*?" This isn't quite the kind of question that you like to hear after spending hours each week preparing what you think is a life-changing Bible study. ("What's wrong with this blockhead?" I thought, but of course I had enough sense not to say it.) But Michael's question is an important one. We often encounter new ideas and have deep discussions, but then we stop short of embodying the faithfulness that we have envisioned. The biblical idea of *knowing* includes our response to what is learned. To truly know something means not simply understanding it, but acting on that understanding.

We don't think you will catapult into academic faithfulness all at once, and we don't think you'll do it simply by reading *about* it. We hope this book launches you on the journey, but we know that the book itself will only play a small role. We think there are some things that you can *do* that will contribute to your development in lasting ways. At some point you've got to get on the bike and ride. (Expect some bruising.) The Nike philosophy for learning is Just Do It. Our philosophy isn't quite as catchy: we want you to do, to imagine, to reflect, to talk, to read, to pray—all of it. But the tag line, "Just do all of it," isn't nearly as catchy as what Nike came up with. In this chapter we are proposing that you will learn deep and significant things as you begin to change your *practices*. It isn't easy to incorporate new practices, new habits and patterns, into your already-overbooked academic life, but it is the only path toward academic faithfulness. Two students, Michael (introduced briefly above) and Maggie, will provide a little input along the way. We hope that you will soon find yourselves walking in their shoes.

Connect Up, Connect Out

The kind of change we have in mind is going to require a little help from those who know and love you. So the first order of business will be strengthening the relationships with those who are in a position to help you most. First and foremost, every Christian ought to be involved in the practices that will help nurture a deep and dynamic relationship with Jesus Christ. We aren't going to spend too much time on these practices, not because we don't think that they are important, but simply because most of the Christian books you have read and most of the Christian input you have received have probably been designed to help you develop good practices in this area.

What does it take to develop and maintain a vibrant relationship with the living Christ? Whether you were a church brat for as long as you can remember or an orphan recently adopted into the family of God, a relationship with Jesus Christ is no static thing. Many of us can remember when it began—a dramatic encounter with Jesus himself. Upon confessing our own sinfulness and calling upon Christ for forgiveness, something happened. We were ushered into some new state, connected to powerful promises, and reanimated with a new Spirit. Perhaps you were super-charged for a time—emotionally elevated by the existential encounter. But at some point even those who had a dramatic conversion experience will come back down to earth to join other Christians who have been confessing their allegiance to Christ since childhood.

Our relationship with Jesus can't rest on the emotional high. It must be nurtured the way any relationship is—by spending time together. And this is what the church is all about. Christians gather together to spend time in relationship with Jesus Christ. Sometimes we miss this in services week after week, but when "church" is done well, important aspects of our relationship with Jesus are rehearsed and celebrated in some kind of weekly gathering.

1. We confess our faith together.
2. We confess our sins together and enjoy the announcement and assurance of our forgiveness in Christ.
3. We celebrate our union with Christ in the sacraments.
4. We sing songs that exalt Jesus and his saving actions on our behalf.
5. We talk to the one we love in prayer—confessing, requesting, adoring.

6. We hear the scriptures read, and then in sermon or homily we explore what Jesus is saying to us in these passages.
7. Little by little we are equipped to obey and serve, to extend the love of Christ and the promise of his kingdom into every aspect of the creation.

Of course, these things shouldn't simply take place for an hour or two each week. Church is the place where we practice these things together as a community. Each one of us needs to carry these practices with us into the routines of everyday life. That Sunday morning relationship with Jesus should be just as real on Monday morning and on through Saturday night. Our relationship with Christ isn't put on hold while we are at work, or while we study, or while we engage in competition. The things that we practice on Sunday morning should be put into practice all week long. I'd be crazy not to delight in the forgiveness proclaimed in the gospel every day. I'd be missing out on something very sweet if I didn't try to carry deep gratitude with me all day long. My relationship with Christ will be shortchanged if I don't follow up that weekly connection to the Bible by connecting to the Bible at other times—in daily readings and in a weekly Bible study. I ought to be working hard to remain connected to Christ all week long, regardless of what I am doing.

Prayer is an essential aspect of *connecting up*, and it is also an aspect that is widely neglected. Even though Christians claim to believe in supernatural realities, many live without any regard for the supernatural, and they doubt that prayer is of any real consequence. I fall into this mindset all too frequently. I say a prayer of thanksgiving when I'm happy, or I ask for guidance when I've got a big decision to make. I *use* prayer. And with that attitude prayer does little to foster the strong relationship that I need most. I too seldom pray in order to connect to Jesus, or to ask him to come with me into other areas of my life. As we have already discussed, the academic world is broken in many places as a result of sin. I know that I need to be in prayer for my school, and I need to ask Jesus to walk with me on campus. Prayer is a vital first step toward academic faithfulness.

Would you be willing to commit yourself to a week-long prayer experiment? Pray for your professors, for your classmates, for your research interests, for wisdom. If you are part of a prayer or Bible study group, pray about taking learning seriously. Pray before each class—a brief prayer will do just fine—and pray before you begin to engage your readings and assignments. We think this is a good place to start the journey of academic faithfulness and something tangible that you can *do*. We also think this experiment will help you to establish an important *practice* that in time will change you. Saying a little prayer like this before a class or before you study would be a good start:

> God, I trust that you have called me to this institution, this major, this class. Help me to discern the lies, to retain valuable insights, and to contribute humbly as I may. I ask for your wisdom as I learn more about your world. Watch over me as I study and engage this material. Through my work here, prepare me to serve in your kingdom.

Connecting up isn't enough. We must also connect out—to other believers. The faith of Lone Ranger Christians is exceedingly fragile and prone to distortion. In addition to the fellowship of the local church mentioned above, Christian students need faithful friends to encourage, stretch, refine, and strengthen them. In order for these friendships to go deep, friends need to spend time together talking about significant things. Maggie expressed it this way:

> God provided me with a good, strong group of Christian friends who stuck with me. Being a Christian on campus is hard, so you need a community to help you through. I knew I couldn't do this alone, especially this work on academic faithfulness. I needed a place to ask questions and throw around ideas. My Christian friends helped me to stay on track. They helped me judge if what I was thinking was biblical. They helped me wrestle with questions related to course material and with bigger questions related to my life and my future.

My experience in college was just like Maggie's. God's best provision for me, and I thank him for it still, was a group of good Christian friends that supported and challenged me throughout college, and then for many years beyond college as well. If I would not have had such a group of friends, I wouldn't have done half the things I did in college—volunteer service, mission trips, leading Bible studies and a campus fellowship group, reading dozens of Christian books, talking with professors after class, debating hard issues late into the night. I am not exaggerating when I say that I learned more in these discussions and activities than I learned in my courses. It is hard for me now, as a professor, to see so many students who are missing the joy and engagement of what college can be precisely because they do not have a vital group of peers that are engaging issues passionately. Of course it does still happen for some. Perhaps God has blessed you in this way. If not, add this to your prayer list and begin to invest in the friendships that will foster your own faithfulness.

Connecting with other Christians is critical, but it isn't the endgame. Christian students should also be connecting in dozens of other ways with all kinds of people. We encourage you to team up with those who are thinking deeply in your discipline and those who are acting courageously in society. Perhaps you ought to consider connecting with

- a professor or mentor who will invest in you
- groups in which the voice of a thoughtful Christian is welcome and needed
- discussion groups in your particular discipline
- a group of volunteers working in your community
- people whose religious beliefs differ from yours
- people whose culture and traditions are widely different from your own

While most colleges and universities do little to help students *connect up*, they are doing a great deal to help students *connect out*. There are probably great opportunities for you to learn beyond the ivy walls of the academy by taking advantage of study abroad opportunities or other kinds of special academic programs. Busting out of the ivory tower through service learning is another important way to learn by doing and to put your faith into action.

Christians are to be like a lamp set on a lamp stand. Imagine some silly town that clustered all of its street lights on the same corner. Christians are to cast light into the gray of night, so they've got to be strategically scattered. Light needs to be shed on all of the streets of God's world, and in particular all along Campus Drive.

Dig Deep, Dig Slow

I had a class in college called *Humanities: Philosophy and the Arts*. It was designed to explore the roots of Western civilization—just the kind of course that students love to hate. In fact, students gave the course a less than affectionate name—*Human Parts*. I remember feeling sorry for the professor. He was passionate and enthusiastic about the class even in the midst of complete student contempt for the course. Poor guy. When students did happen to come to class, you could tell that they would rather be anywhere else. There was PlayStation to be played.

Many college students simply endure time in class. Apparently those who don't show up can't even endure it, or perhaps they do not value the experience very highly. But should this be true for Christians? In retrospect, my response to my *Human Parts* class frustrates me. I hated and endured it just like every other student. I wasted over $1000 of tuition and about 180 hours of my time, and I squandered the opportunity to know a little something about the roots and fruits of Western culture. Ironically, this is the stuff that now interests me most. I wish I would have paid attention to what was being taught. All I would have needed to do was to listen and to invest a little more of my energy in the reading, discussions, and assignments. I guess I resented being forced to take a class that I didn't want. In the end I really only hurt myself.

Theologian John Stott has written an important book pleading with Christians to become better listeners. He writes, "One of the most important—and much neglected—ingredients of Christian discipleship is the cultivation of a listening ear. Bad listeners do not make good disciples." And bad listeners do not make good students.

I don't mean just listening to teachers in order to know what is going to be on the test in order to get a good grade. Good students listen to what is being said, and they listen between the lines. They hear what isn't being said and listen for what could or should be said. Academic faithfulness requires a listening ear.

After you have prayed and paid attention in class, it is time to probe. The topics of our texts and lectures need to be subjected to penetrating scrutiny. We need to nurture our own curiosity and critical inquiry in order to get to the heart of important issues and to understand those issues in their broader cultural and creational context. Good students explore their own academic discipline and the connections between their discipline and other disciplines, and deeper still, the connections between their learning and their faith. Consequently, Christian students desiring to be faithful to Christ will have some extra work to do. This won't be easy. Stott suggests that students need to engage in "double listening." Christians need to listen to both the Word and the world:

> We listen to the Word with humble reverence, anxious to understand it, and resolved to believe and obey what we come to understand. We listen to the world with critical alertness, anxious to understand it too, and resolved not necessarily to believe and obey it, but to sympathize with it and to seek grace to discover how the gospel relates to it.

It starts by learning to ask good questions about what we are studying. Brian Walsh gets things rolling in his article "Christian + University = ?":

> Why is economics generally reduced to a quantitative science? What is at stake in the synthesis of music and

technology in much contemporary music? What fundamental assumptions about being human are at the root of conflicting schools of thought in psychology (behaviorism, Freudian psychoanalysis, transactional analysis, bioenergetics)? Why does science play the most formative role in the health professions? Should it have such a role? Why does the engineering department view technology as the true route to social blessing? What presuppositions are entailed in such a faith? How does the social work department define social well-being? All of these questions point to the world view roots of university study. Christians should be asking such questions.

There is almost no way an 18-year-old freshman could begin to answer these questions on her own. Digging deep takes us back to connecting. We need to develop and participate in communities that are asking tough questions.

A classic text that links the gospel of Jesus Christ to the things of the world can be found in the book of Colossians. In Colossians 1:15–20 Paul is rhapsodic, describing Jesus's lordship over all things. In fact, in this short passage the word "things" appears seven times. The passage is printed below, but we have replaced the word "things" with an academic word, "disciplines." We've also replaced the broad focus of "heaven and earth" with just one aspect of the creation, "university." We think we are staying true to the spirit of the text as we add a little academic twist.

> Jesus Christ is the image of the invisible God, the firstborn of all creation; for in him every discipline of the university was created, disciplines visible and invisible, whether thrones or dominions or rulers or powers—all disciplines have been created through him and for him. He himself is before all disciplines, and in him all disciplines hold together. He is the head of the body, the church; he is the

beginning, the firstborn from the dead, so that he might come to have first place in every discipline. For in him all the fullness of God was pleased to dwell, and through him God was pleased to reconcile to himself every discipline of the university, by making peace through the blood of his cross. (Colossians 1:15–20; academically twisted)

There is so much to dig into. Every discipline of the academy and every corner of the creation are ours to explore. And not only is Jesus the work-boss, he is the architect and builder and completer of this project that we are working on. My point here is simply that Christian students ought to dig in and pay attention in the classes that they have. This is a *practice*. Some of you already embody this practice, but for many of us this is going to require real effort.

Anyone who has ever attempted to dig a deep hole in hard ground knows that if you want to finish the job, you'd better dig slowly. Digging isn't some kind of crazy race to see who can dig the deepest well or the longest ditch. It won't do any good to develop blisters in the first ten minutes of work or to run out of steam after twenty. Academic digging isn't a race either, but in time you'll find that you've moved plenty of earth. If you engage in the practices of prayer, paying attention, and probing, it is perfectly fine to pace yourself and be patient. (*OK, enough with the "p" words!*) Rome wasn't built in a day, and neither is the faithful Christian student.

Late in college, I had a chip on my shoulder the size of Delaware. I think I had decided that the secular bias of the academy needed to be confronted in the classroom and that I was just the crusader to do it. The trouble was I generally knew almost nothing about the subjects being discussed. I was courageous, and speaking up was good for me. Unfortunately, however, my efforts did little to display a thoughtful Christian perspective and to persuade other students or professors that Christians had anything to offer. Several times I hijacked classroom conversation in an attempt to evangelize my professors. It's not that academic faithfulness will not be evangelistic per se, it's just that we need to be careful with our attitude. We need to practice patience. I had a lot of reading and learning to do before I had much to contribute in most of these conversations. And at that time I had no intention of really doing my homework. I needed to learn that God wasn't placing the burden of the university on my narrow shoulders in a 9:00 a.m. biology lecture on evolution. The world was not in danger of ending if a professor ardently claimed that God did not exist in Philosophy 201.

There will be times to take a stand for Christ in the classroom, no doubt, and the courage of Christian students will be tested in the classroom. But patience and humility must also be practiced—for your sake, for the sake of others in the classroom, and for the sake of the gospel itself. Pray, pay attention, learn to ask good questions, and relax. Be patient. Proceed with quiet confidence. And don't be surprised when God shows up, providing plenty of opportunities for you to bear witness to "the firstborn of all creation."

Discussion Questions

1. The biblical idea of *knowing* includes our response to what is learned. Why is this important to keep in mind?
2. What are some of the practices that help you nurture your relationship with Jesus Christ? Are you stronger in some areas than in others?

3. Why is prayer essential to academic faithfulness?
   Are you willing to commit yourself to the week-long
   prayer experiment mentioned in this chapter?
4. We mention about six different kinds of relationships that we think are vital for academic faithfulness.
   What are they? How many of them do you currently
   have? Do you have any ideas of how to pursue the
   others?
5. Read Colossians 1:15–20 and insert your major in
   place of "things." Does this sound right to you?

Recommendations

Henri J. M. Nouwen, *Reaching Out: The Three Movements of the Spiritual Life* (New York: Image Books, 1986).

Dallas Willard, *The Spirit of the Disciplines: Understanding How God Changes Lives* (San Francisco: HarperSanFrancisco, 1991).

N. T. Wright, *For All God's Worth: True Worship and the Calling of the Church* (Grand Rapids: Eerdmans, 1997).

CHUTES AND LADDERS

CHAPTER 8

When we were kids we used to love a game called Chutes and Ladders. We loved it because it was simple, and it was also full of little surprises. All you do in this game is roll the dice and try to move from the bottom to the top of the game board. Some rolls land your plastic piece at the base of a ladder. When this occurs, you automatically zip through layers of the game toward victory. But if your piece moves to a square at the top of a chute, or sliding board, you slide back down the board closer again to the start. Simple—and a bit like life.

Life is full of ups and downs. That's been my experience in the Christian life as well. I've had some weeks (and months and even years) in which I felt that God was really at work in me. I'd be inching along in life's game, landing on more than my share of ladders along the way. During these times I'd experience bursts of growth, sort of spiritual quantum leaps. During these times the Christian life always felt unpredictable, but in a good, exhilarating way. I've gone through other periods in which life was all chutes and setbacks. I hate those darn chutes, and I hate those periods in my life in which I feel stagnant and unproductive and, well, lousy. I try to keep on moving my piece forward, square by square, but I feel like I'm slipping backward. God feels distant and life feels unpredictable. During these times the unpredictability feels debilitating, not exhilarating.

Faithfulness is mostly a matter of inching in the right direction. Sometimes God catapults us forward, and sometimes we feel as if we are moving in exactly the wrong direction. Even though it sometimes feels like a game or a roller coaster, the Christian life is really more like a walk. Kosuke Koyama has written a book called *Three Mile an Hour God: Biblical Reflections*. Three miles per hour is the pace of easy walking, the kind of walk on which you can carry on a good conversation. The three mph God is, you guessed it, Jesus himself. Throughout the Gospels he is walking everywhere, and all along the way he is talking to the disciples and other travelers he meets along the way. Three mph is still the preferred pace of Jesus. He seems to be interested in getting to know us at a very human pace, and it appears that we are best connected to one another at about that same pace. If we are running everywhere we go, we shouldn't expect relationships to flourish, and if we don't get up and get moving, we shouldn't expect much then either. We need to keep one another heading in the right direction, and we need to remind one another that the tortoise was mostly right—slow and steady is the pace of faithfulness.

Herbie was introduced in an earlier chapter. In the last chapter you briefly encountered two other students, Michael and Maggie. You are going to have an opportunity to hear a good bit more from these two in this chapter. We aren't giving these students press to make them feel good. And we aren't highlighting them because they are exceptional students. All three were simply seeking to be faithful college students. We hope that you will have stories like theirs to tell.

Maggie, how have you worked to incorporate your Christian faith in the classroom?
The classroom can be an intimidating place. Before I became a Christian, I remember thinking, "What do I have to

contribute? The professor has a Ph.D. and has been thinking about this stuff for years." My thoughts began to change when I became a Christian. I slowly began to recognize that the Bible speaks to all of life. If certain philosophies and lifestyles contradicted it, I needed to be aware of it, instead of mindlessly consuming it. For me it was learning how to obey Jesus in my studies, not simply fighting for the A. I remember lying in bed one night reading Romans 12:1–2. It was reassuring to know that a "renewing of the mind" was supposed to take place, because I knew I was changing. The changes in me were scary to me and to my Mom and Dad. At first they feared that I was getting too radical, too Christian, I guess. It would have been easier on me and my parents if I simply held the same course, you know, toward a good job and secure life. But that was no longer my main goal.

This sounds good, but what did you actually do differently?

I began to take time to think carefully about what I was learning. For instance, in my religion course, I began to think about why other people believe the things that they believe, and why I believe the things that I believe. This kind of thinking led to dozens of interesting conversations. When I had to pick an essay theme for a literature class, I looked for themes related to faith or belief or values. I wanted to write about something of deep significance. During the unit on evolution in bio, I asked about the viability of intelligent design theory. Later in that same course, during a discussion on stem cell research, I was asked by the professor how the Christian faith might inform the debate. The professor actually treated me like some kind of expert. I was embarrassed to admit that I had no idea, but being asked sparked something in me. From that point on I wanted to be prepared to offer some evidence that Christianity makes a difference in the way I think about contemporary issues.

Read Twice, Write Thrice

Academic faithfulness is not easy. We said it would be a meaningful adventure, but we never said it would be a breeze. Some of the things mentioned in the previous chapter don't take a lot of extra time; they simply require extra effort. Replacing daydreaming disinterest in a class with attentive curiosity is simply a matter a focus. Bending conversations with your friends away from highlights of a recent TV show to the implications of an old theory or a new technology takes passion and practice, but it doesn't require additional study time. But now I've got to level with you: you are a double major of sorts. To do justice to your studies, you will need to study not only the subject matter at hand like everybody else, you will also need to study the scriptures and the works of other informed Christian scholars who have explored the subject matter that is in view. Most of your college courses won't introduce a Christian perspective or require reading of Christian authors. You are going to have to do this on your own or with that small band of Christian friends who are also taking academic faithfulness seriously.

American evangelicals have been mesmerized by an anti-intellectual spirit for nearly a century now. No doubt you and I have inherited some of the bad practices and bad ideas of our own Christian heritage. But there is good news as well. In many sectors of the academy, Christians have been thoughtfully and courageously engaging in Christian scholarship. Many brilliant Christian professors are teaching in America's colleges and universities, and more and more they are seeing their work as a professor as a call to profess not only facts within their discipline but also the faith-anchored framework that makes sense of the facts.

Brilliant Christian scholars are also writing books (as they always have), but more and more of these works are being recognized as significant contributions to the academic debates of our day.

Christian students need to do their part by participating in this intellectual awakening. Christian students should be reading more than their non-Christian roommates, and in fact, I believe that they have a deeper motivation for taking learning seriously. The Christian student seeks to honor the Lord of learning. "Double study" is going to take a little extra time, and it will cost a little extra money. Double study is also the hard work that is going to prepare you to be the kind of person who can take your faith with you into the classroom without embarrassment. Even more important, double study will prepare you to take your faith with you beyond college, into your life and work.

One obstacle to engaging in double study needs to be addressed, and that is identifying and finding the right books to read. Exactly what the "right" book is may depend on your own theological tradition, and it will certainly depend on what you are studying. This is where a Christian mentor can really come in handy, but even seasoned Christians have often neglected reading deeply and broadly enough to help enquiring students. A local Christian bookstore may be a good place to start, but unfortunately many of these bookstores do not contain Christian books that address academic issues. Instead, they carry popular books about the Christian life and self-help books designed to encourage Christians to lose weight, manage their money, improve their marriage, become a leader, or homeschool their children. You are going to need a better guide to the books that will help you develop a Christian perspective in the academic arena. We don't provide a bibliography of titles by discipline right here in this book, partly because new resources are being made available every week. If you want to peruse a good bibliography, come to www.academicfaithulness.com. We'll keep it up to date for you, and we'll provide a forum for you to ask some questions about topics you are working on as well. We will also recommend some of our favorite places to buy books (with discounts!).

Michael said it. "If it wasn't for my classes, I would love college!" After about a year of getting to know him, we started to meet regularly to study God's Word. In one of our initial conversations, I told Michael the story of how Bach used to sign his written music *Soli Deo Gloria* or with the abbreviation S.D.G. It means "to God alone be the glory." Whether the piece was for church worship or for popular entertainment, Bach tried to honor God through his work. I asked Michael, "Do you sign your college papers and exams S.D.G.?" Perplexed, and rightfully so (I mean, come on, who talks about Bach?), Michael responded, "You know, I don't really care about my classes. There are other things more important than learning about obscure things." The more we talked, the more Michael realized that he should take his academics seriously, because, as we discussed, all things are important to God and we should do all things for his glory.

Over the next month or so something unexpected happened. Michael began to care about his academic work. I'm always challenging students, but so few really follow through, so I was surprised. Michael was working on a final paper for a political science course on the differing views on abortion of two presidential candidates. It was the best paper he ever wrote. He knew it, and he was rightly proud of his work. In the paper, Michael summarized the candidates' views very well; he offered his own well-rounded insight and critique of the issue—and for all of his effort, he was accused of plagiarism! Michael had never written like this before, and the professor couldn't believe that it was actually his work. Michael explained to the professor, "No, I started to care about the topic, and I really wanted it give it my best effort." After that conversation, the prof was convinced, and a relationship between Michael and the prof developed. Michael also began to develop an interest in public policy that led him to an internship in Washington, D.C. To this day his interest in public policy and his commitment to think faithfully about his work have not abated. *Soli Deo Gloria!*

Becoming a good writer requires hard work. In my early years of college my papers were returned to me covered in blood-colored ink. I knew I wasn't a good speller, and I wasn't a careful proofreader. It took me a while to realize that I needed a great deal of help on basic grammar and essay construction as well. Apparently I had missed the only teacher in high school that really trained students in the mechanics of good writing. If you need help sharpening your writing skills, now is the time to get it. You may want to take advantage of your campus writing center or find a writing coach, someone patient and willing to help you learn to write clearly. Being able to communicate well in writing is going to help you in most of your college courses. It will give you confidence in communicating your views orally as well, and it will pay dividends for you beyond college. Don't be embarrassed if you haven't already been well trained. This is very common, and you can begin to address your writing skills on your next assignment.

Many of you are already passable writers, and some even have a real talent for it. The challenge for you is to consider writing for a threefold audience. First of all, you will need to keep your eye on the assignment itself. Your first audience is the professor and the particular question or topic under consideration. Thinking Christianly about a topic does not give a student the freedom to wander away from the assigned topic. But writing a good paper addressing the topic is only the beginning.

Your second audience is Jesus Christ himself. You should be writing in such a way that the Lord would pronounce that wonderful benediction over your work, "Well done, good and faithful servant." This does not mean that the paper should become a sermon or a theological treatise. It means that what you have written reflects deep and faithful attention to the subject at hand, while at the same time reflecting your own view, a faith-informed view, of the subject. What this entails will certainly be different from paper to paper, and you will likely need to tap the resources of your peer group or a mentor to help you frame your response. How does your Christian faith shape your view of this topic? Is a distinctively Christian response warranted?

Good writers should consider a third audience as well—a public audience. As a professor, I've seen so much good work done by students, so much deep thought and faithful reflection, and I know that I am the only person that ever reads these papers. Sometimes I encourage students to publish what they have written in the school paper, an on-campus journal, or a blog. Some of my colleagues take students to conferences to present papers, and a few students have had their work published in academic journals. To share good work is not only an academic expression of "loving one's neighbor," it is also a good practice for students seeking to develop a public voice.

At this point in your academic journey this may sound a little overwhelming. Here is a less threatening way to get started, and several students I know launched this little experiment just last semester. The students planned a bi-monthly forum in which a dozen or so students convened to hear one of the students read a paper he or she had written. The students would also invite a faculty member or two (not too many) who knew something about the topic being addressed and would be able to provide some kind of Christian reflection on the topic. So far the papers I've heard have been fantastic, and the discussion about the papers has been more valuable than anything that I can do in a normal class session. Students plan it, they present, and they discuss. If the faculty members are wise, they will contribute a little, but mostly they will sit back and watch God at work in the midst of a group of students who are experiencing something remarkable. Being part of two of these sessions was the highlight of my work on campus last semester.

Dream Big, Act Small

Two things can happen to a college student, and both of these things are very bad. Unfortunately, both are also very common. You can lose the capacity to dream, and you can lose the gumption to act. Students need to have big dreams to help them work hard throughout college. We already argued in chapter one that one kind of dream, Grades and Accolades, is a dead end. Many students imagine that their academic success will lead to success on the job and that this success on the job will lead to happiness in life. Most of us are motivated at least a little by that American Dream. But what if you aren't getting the grades? Or what if your dream job, say, helping impoverished families, won't buy the American Dream? What if you've begun to feel that the dream isn't all it's cracked up to be?

Brea, a senior occupational therapy student, was searching for a new dream, for something to make sense of her studies and her future aspirations. At a weekly Bible study she asked us to pray for her: "Please pray for me. I'm feeling a lot of stress, and I'm not sure why. It's not like I have more work this semester than normal. I just don't know why I am learning what I am learning. I feel like if there was a reason for what I am learning, any reason beyond to get a grade, then I could work hard again. But in all of my classes, I can't honestly tell you why I need to learn this stuff. I have no idea why this matters." Brea wants her learning to matter. She senses that there must be more to learning than "getting the grade."

Brea had several good friends who prayed for her and wrestled with her very sincere questions. I haven't heard that many students put feelings of academic frustration into words like Brea did, but I've seen students struggle and cry and get mad and give up because they felt almost exactly the same way. Meaninglessness is the disease, and it just might be an epidemic on campus. Proverbs 29:18 reminds us that where there is no vision, people lose their way. That certainly appears to be true for college students as well. If you don't know why you're attending college, there is a good chance that you will struggle and eventually lose your way.

I always envied (and secretly despised) kids who knew exactly what they wanted to be when they grew up. I know a few who have never wavered from their precocious certainty. I thought I found it once—that kind of certainty. When I was seven, I saw a television special with oceanographer Jacques Cousteau. I was so certain that I should be an oceanographer that I had my Dad write that one word—oceanographer—on a tiny piece of paper. (I was too young to spell it, and a notoriously bad speller to boot.) I took that small reminder and put it inside a wallet that I had received for Christmas that year. Why a seven-year-old needs a wallet, I have no idea. I wouldn't have a driver's license or folding money for ten years. But I figured that right about the time that I'd need that wallet I'd also need to be reminded about the precise nature of my life's work.

Well, since that time so long ago I've wanted to be a lot of things—a forest ranger, a doctor, an optometrist, a physicist, a pastor, a bush pilot, a professor, and a fishing guide. So far I can only mark two off my list, but I don't think my list of aspirations is finished yet. And yours may not be either. In the midst of changing ambitions and possibilities, something deep and powerful needs to be discovered. And that is this: No matter what you finally decide to do, you cannot do it to please someone else, and you cannot do it to please yourself. You'll finally be satisfied only when your personal dreams and ambitions are connected to the purposes of God in the restoration of his creation. At least that has been my experience, and it was Maggie's experience too.

Maggie, you seem passionate about academic faithfulness.

I am. This kind of faithfulness is so rarely practiced but so desperately needed. While studying to be a teacher, I realized that I would be a better teacher if I took my courses seriously. And, of course, I came to realize that being a good teacher will benefit not only me, but it will benefit the children as well. I believe that God wants good teachers who are committed to developing good schools and to reaching out to students who need good training and coaching and encouraging.

One thing I realized is that it means loving God with all he has given me, including my mind. This might sound strange, but I think about what it means to be a blessing to others. No, better, I think about the Lord's Prayer—on earth as it is in heaven. I want to see heaven come to earth. Somehow I think that my work in the classroom can help in God's restoration of the earth. My preparation to teach, and eventually my work as a teacher, is fueled by my belief in the kingdom of God. I believe that the reign of Jesus in his creation has begun, and that I am to be part of it.

Now that is a big dream, and Maggie is quite able to connect her own sense of vocation and purpose with the biblical story of God's redemptive love. Some of you have already been overwhelmed by truly worthy dreams—urban restoration, AIDs research, racial reconciliation, child welfare, legal reform. It isn't easy pursuing justice or embodying compassion or seeking cures in the face of overwhelming need. The areas of greatest need in the world are often neglected precisely because Christian students can't imagine making a dent in the problem. We hesitate to step into tough service because we can't really imagine the success of the undertaking. It might help if we reminded one another from time to time that success isn't our mission, faithfulness is. God will bring success in time, and it will be colossal and complete.

For dreams to shake us and to move us, they've got to grow legs. They have to be put to work in the world. I've known many students who dreamed worthy dreams, who talked a good game, and yet they never really lived up to all the talk. This has been true even (especially?) of Christian students and their God-talk. Developing a theology of the kingdom is crucial, but it is just as important to begin to live out the implications of that theology. And that is why it is so important to begin now to *act small*, to begin to engage in small acts of faithfulness even if the response feels meager and insignificant compared to the big dream.

- While you can't stop children from being abandoned by their parents, you could become a Big Brother or a Big Sister.
- Yes, literacy is a huge problem with lasting repercussions. So instead of ignoring the issue, perhaps you could tutor a couple of children in a nearby school.
- Will developing a recycling program in your residence hall make a difference? The benefit may be small, but even small acts of stewardship begin to establish concerns and patterns of faithful living that will last a lifetime.
- Let's say that in your poli-sci class you were convinced about the danger of eroding civic engagement. What would you do, in the course and beyond, as first steps toward responsible citizenship? Sadly, most of us do nothing at all.

We think that during your college experience you should engage in a wide range of ministries, community volunteer programs, and organizations committed to social justice. By engaging in a number of different activities, you will be connected to people and programs that will remind you of the wide array of ways to faithfully serve God. We all need to be reminded that we are called to faithfulness, not just in one area of life, but in all areas. That certainly doesn't mean that we will be able to join every available ministry and program. In fact, in time you will likely find that there are some kinds of investment and service that really suit you, and in these areas you may be able to provide leadership and to recruit others to join you in service. So in addition to engaging in a wide range of activities, you'll probably discover a few issues that you will want to pour yourself into. That's good. That's the way the body of Christ works. Paul says it like this in 1 Corinthians 12:

> There are different kinds of gifts, but the same Spirit. There are different kinds of service, but the same Lord. . . . The body is a unit, though it is made up of many parts; and though all its parts are many, they form one body. (vv. 4, 5, 12)

Not everyone is an eyeball or a nose or an elbow. Some parts will serve in some ways, and other parts will perform different duties. But all parts are to remain united under the head, Jesus Christ. Right now I'm trying to be the hand that beckons you to faithful engagement, or perhaps the hand that is giving you a little shove in the right direction.

There's another way to "act small" that has huge consequences. Every Christian student who has stepped into the exciting adventure of living and studying faithfully ought to drag someone else along. When we share the vision with another, and when we encourage another to explore daily faithfulness, even academic faithfulness, we will be following the pattern displayed for us by Jesus himself.

Work Hard, Play Hard

I know that we've already said it many times. Academic faithfulness is hard work. In fact, you're probably convinced by now that it is outrageous! We hope you aren't one to back down from a big challenge. Michael didn't back down, and he loved the ongoing challenges of academic faithfulness.

Michael, you're a senior now. Tell me what it means to put the two words together, academic and faithfulness.
Jesus says that we are to love God with all our heart and soul and mind and strength. That's all I'm trying to do, love with my mind. It means signing all my papers and homework to the glory of God. [Where did he hear that crazy idea?] It means trying to see and understand the world the way God does. I want to honor God by using the gifts that I've been given, and I want to use them in and beyond the classroom.

Michael, is academic faithfulness hard work?
Yeah, it is hard. Academic faithfulness is not simply going to church while you are in college. It's hard because I have to have a strong understanding of both my faith and the subject I am studying. Often I don't feel like my understanding of either is strong enough. I have to read my textbooks and study Christian books, like, all the time. I have to look at a textbook and ask: "What are the implications of my faith on what I am reading?"

Congratulations are in order. You recently won an award for a paper you wrote. How did you do it?
Well, first, I'm pretty stubborn, and I didn't want to give up. I started by reading good books and asking a lot of questions. You need to be willing to study hard and ask tough questions. I committed time to the project and asked for feedback—from several good friends and interested professors.

What has surprised you most about your academic journey?
Not that it is hard work. I knew that. But that it has actually been a lot of fun. Before I met you, I would write a

paper by taking every shortcut I could imagine. I didn't cheat, but mostly what I did was cut and paste from various sources. Now I think about being faithful. I dig deeper, think harder, and try to say something worthwhile. It's fulfilling. When I'm finished, I feel that in some small way I have made a difference. Somehow this will be used by God. At least, I guess, it is helping to shape me into the person God wants me to be. Studying hard and writing well is good preparation for being used by God.

By working hard to honor God, you just might find that you are actually enjoying him as well. That's what God really wants—not just your determined obedience, but your delight and wonder and curiosity and compassion. If your capacity for delight and wonder and curiosity and compassion is being enlarged while you are in college, then that is a very good sign indeed. For one thing, that is what most of us really want for ourselves. Academic faithfulness is the sure cure for collegiate boredom, apathy, and listlessness. I wouldn't have had half as much fun in college if I hadn't been exploring the kingdom vision of the scriptures along with my friends. Second, once you begin to display these qualities, others will want to get in on the action too. You'll be able to begin discussion groups, share books, and attend conferences together. Fellowship will erupt, and that will lead to another thing that most of us want—good community. A third thing as well: as you begin to display these qualities, God will be honored, and I think we can say too that God will be delighted.

Pursuing faithfulness at college won't be easy, but it's a good struggle. This pursuit is what made college an adventure for Michael, and he has continued on that hard-working yet playful adventure in graduate school. Michael learned that faithful writing is marked S.D.G., whether he writes it at the end of his papers or not. Of course the Hallelujah chorus doesn't break out whenever he hands in a paper, but I imagine that a divine "Yes" is whispered. There is a strain of worship in academic work done well. God is honored when he is recognized as the source of all good things, the one who holds all things together, and the one who will someday make all things right.

Discussion Questions

1. Why is practicing patience important? What potential dangers exist if we are not patient?
2. In this chapter we ask you to consider three audiences when writing academic papers. What audience do you generally consider?
3. Have you ever worked at something so diligently, something that you even brought your beliefs to bear upon, that you would be willing to mark it S.D.G?
4. What are some of your big dreams? What are some small acts of faithfulness that you could pursue to make those dreams a reality?
5. Do you suppose that God is interested in our play and recreation as much as in our work and study?

Recommendations

Richard Mouw, *When the Kings Come Marching In: Isaiah and the New Jerusalem*, rev. ed. (Grand Rapids: Eerdmans, 2002).

George M. Marsden, *The Outrageous Idea of Christian Scholarship* (New York: Oxford University Press, 1998).

CONCLUSION

College is weird. It has always seemed strange to me that just when students have big decisions to make and need guidance most, college tears them away from the social networks (family, church, friends) that could provide the support that they need. Fortunately, many of us made good friends in the first few months of college, and eventually perhaps we found trusted mentors to guide and support us. But many others feel incredibly isolated and lonely.

The proverbial college "bubble" is a little weird too. College campuses are veritable utopias. When you want to eat, you go to any number of locations around campus, swipe a card that has been loaded with electronic money, and eat to your heart's content. Students everywhere complain about the food, but I've eaten on many campuses, and I'd choose more than a few over my mother's cooking. In addition to this convenience, students have access to state-of-the-art exercise facilities. Most don't realize that this kind of access will cost them hundreds of dollars each year after college. Students can stay up all night, and they can sleep in all day if they want to. All kinds of events and activities are planned that are designed just for them. No doubt many of you are working your way through college. But many others have yet to hold a significant job. The bubble will soon burst, and all this will end. Other than a hefty debt, what will the graduate be carrying into the post-bubble world?

I guess the main reason that I think college is weird is that it isn't designed to help us become what we really need to become. So much that goes on during the college years is irrelevant, shallow, and even destructive. I think that was Tom Wolfe's point in *I Am Charlotte Simmons: A Novel*. Don't get me wrong; I think life and college should be full of laughter and plenty of good times. It just seems to me that all of that time (4+ years) and all that money ($25K to $175K) could be put to much better use.

All of that said, I wouldn't trade my four years of college back even if my alma mater could reimburse every penny and every minute. College is a colossal opportunity. I encountered life-shaping people and engaged in life-shaping activities there, and I developed views and abilities and relationships for which I am profoundly thankful. God guided me to a good church and provided me with an engaging group of Christian friends, a mentor, and several excellent faculty members. The same thing can happen for you. It will not happen because of some ingenious educational reform. Your college or university will not provide what you need most. Good experiences and deep learning depend on decisions that you will make and the investment that you make in your own learning.

As you start into the adventure called college, we think you should follow the example of Joshua and Caleb. Part of their story is recorded in Numbers 13. At this point in history Israel had been released from bondage in Egypt and the nation had sojourned to the border regions of the

Promised Land. A rep from each of the twelve tribes of Israel was chosen to sneak in and spy out the land. The spies discovered that the land was fertile and fruitful. In fact, they described it as a "land flowing with milk and honey," and they brought back baskets of produce to display to the Israelites. But that's not all they reported. The land was also full of stout people and strong cities. Ten spies gave a discouraging report to the Israelites: "We don't stand a chance. That land will devour us! The people are so mighty (even the giant Nephilim are there!) that we felt like tiny grasshoppers before them." Evidently Joshua and Caleb were more impressed by God's promise than they were by the opposition. They said, "We should go up and take possession of the land, for we can certainly do it."

The Promised Land isn't the only piece of real estate that belongs to God. The whole earth is God's, including every college and university in the world. You are being sent on a mission yourself. Like a good spy, take a look around and see what's going on. You'll notice intellectual giants in the land, and perhaps more than a few strongholds. You may feel like a grasshopper, but don't be afraid. As Joshua and Caleb did long ago, remember God's promise and provision. Carry with you the good report of God's faithfulness. Joshua and Caleb believed that despite appearances, God could do what he had promised. While God hasn't promised to redeem higher education in our day, we have every reason to believe that he has creation-wide restoration in view. And he has promised to be with you wherever you go.

I remember a little footbridge over Wolf Creek that I used to cross on the way to school. I don't know whether it was local vandals or bridge trolls at work, but one day I noticed that the bridge had been tagged. On the four steps this message was painted, one word on each riser: THIS BRIDGE IS OURS! It is risky business to lay claim to some aspect of the creation that belongs to God. It is much more prudent to acknowledge that every inch made by God has been tagged for him in Christ. Everything belongs to God, and everything in the creation is being reclaimed.

One last tagging story. Down the hill from my freshman hall was a lake and a huge boulder. Frats and sororities and other campus groups continuously claimed the rock by tagging it with their letters. In my day it was coated in at least an inch of paint. Claiming the rock seemed like fun, so one night under the cover of darkness we set out to claim the rock. But we were freshman, unaffiliated at the time, and all we could think to do was tag the boulder with its generic name, THE ROCK. We had no other allegiance to announce. Tagging rocks is child's play. The game we have been describing in this book is much more serious—tagging things academic, and tagging them this way—S.D.G.

Recommendations

Quentin J. Schultz, *Here I Am: Now What on Earth Should I Be Doing?* (Grand Rapids: Baker, 2005).

John Piper, *Don't Waste Your Life* (Wheaton, IL: Crossway, 2003).

Os Guinness, *The Call: Finding and Fulfilling the Central Purpose of Your Life* (Nashville: W Publishing Group, 1998).

STUDENT RESPONSES

The Jubilee Conference (www.jubileeconference.com) is an annual gathering of college students to explore the implications of the gospel of the kingdom. Students are challenged not only to enjoy the full embrace of God's love in Christ but also to begin to envision their lives as thoughtful expressions of that love in every area of life. Last year we had the opportunity to talk in small groups with about two hundred of these students about academic faithfulness. We were bowled over by their keen perceptiveness about this challenge, their honesty about their own neglect of academic faithfulness, and their earnest desire to begin the adventure. We've listed some of the comments of these students under two organizing questions below. You may wish to edit and extend the lists to describe your own situation.

What are the key obstacles to academic faithfulness?

1. My own time management and disorganization.
2. I'm so busy. That Facebook is addictive.

3. I don't care enough about my classes.
4. I'm afraid of being persecuted for being a Christian.
5. My own anti-intellectualism.
6. I've compartmentalized my faith.
7. The tyranny of the résumé. I feel pressured to prepare for *the job*.
8. There aren't that many models of students who are doing it.
9. I'm lazy, and I procrastinate.
10. I need a vision of why it matters.
11. There are too many distractions at school, too many other things to do.
12. I hate my prof, or I hate this course.
13. My friends keep me from it. They don't care, so I don't.
14. It's sin. I don't care enough, and I can't even imagine what to do.
15. Gradism. I care more about good grades than faithfulness.
16. Cheating. It's everywhere, and it's so easy to cheat.
17. I'm afraid of the challenge.

What practices would lead you toward academic faithfulness?

1. I should read more books that explore a Christian perspective.
2. Meet with professors during office hours or at other times.
3. Learn to ask foundational questions.
4. Ask for help when I need it.
5. Go to class! And pay attention!
6. Pray regularly about my studies.

7. I need accountability to help me stick with it.
8. I've got to set a schedule that includes double study.
9. I need an academic mentor, especially someone in my field.
10. I must become willing to be different.
11. I've got to choose to love learning.
12. I need to see more clearly how faith is related to my academic work.
13. Post my room with faith-reminders like Colossians 3:17.
14. Have discussions after class with my classmates.
15. I've got to be willing to push beyond the minimum.
16. Stop complaining about my profs and the work I have to do.
17. Humility. Don't act like a know-it-all.

Good start. Now where will you go from here?

REFERENCES

Chapter 1—Wide-Eyed

15   "Once again we are borrowing a title from a book, this one by Murray Sperber.": Murray Sperber, *Beer and Circus: How Big-time College Sports Is Crippling Undergraduate Education* (New York: Owl Books, 2001).

16   "Tom Wolfe provides a particularly poignant portrait of Beer and Circus college life in his recent book *I Am Charlotte Simmons: A Novel*.": Tom Wolfe, *I Am Charlotte Simmons: A Novel* (New York: Farrar, Straus & Giroux, 2004).

Chapter 2—Babylon U

26   "When you go out in the world, watch out for traffic, hold hands and stick together.": Robert Fulghum, *All I Really Need to Know I Learned in Kindergarten* (New York: Ballantine Books, 2003).

28   "We need to recognize the danger of deceptive philosophies and traditions and to advance in our collegiate journey with care and courage.": Paul is up against *it* in the letter to Colossae. What exactly it is is a matter of some debate. Evidently religious innovators are afoot. Chapter two reveals that these innovators are attacking the gospel of Christ, arguing instead for a religion built on human tradition and wisdom and secret revelations from angels. Paul counters their teaching by emphasizing the supremacy of Christ. Jesus himself, Paul argues, is the source of "complete understanding," the one "in whom are hidden all the treasures of wisdom and knowledge" (Colossians 2:2–3). Paul warns the Christians of Colossae not to be duped by the arguments of deceivers. They are particularly warned not to be taken captive by 1) hollow and deceptive philosophy, 2) human tradition,

and 3) principles of the world. The Christians at Colossae aren't the only ones who face false teaching. False teaching filled the ancient world, and it is brimming over in our world today. Paul's caution applies to us as it did to them: Stay sharp. Remain rooted in Christ. Think deeply and carefully about the issues of the day.

32   "On the plain of Dura he erected a golden image of himself that was 90 feet high and 9 feet wide.": The connection between this great totem in Daniel 3 and the statue of Nebuchadnezzar's dream in chapter two is not clear, but Nebuchadnezzar may be trying to reassert his own immortality and that of his kingdom against the interpretation of the dream Daniel had given to him.

Chapter 3—Believing Is Seeing

42   "I believe in germs and justice and gravity, not by sight but because I've heard about them, I see that others believe in them, and they make sense out of many of the things I have experienced.": I know that I could *see* germs if I wanted to. I could find a microscope and spit on a slide. But the point is, I haven't done this and yet I still believe in those pesky little microbes.

43   "The history and development of the notion are discussed in other places, and that doesn't need to concern us here.": See David Naugle, *Worldview: The History of a Concept* (Grand Rapids: Eerdmans, 2002).

43   "a commitment, a fundamental orientation of the heart, that can be expressed as a story or in a set of presuppositions": James Sire, *The Universe Next Door*, 4th ed. (Downers Grove, IL: InterVarsity Press, 2004), 17.

43   "a comprehensive framework of one's beliefs about things that function as a guide to life": Albert Wolters, *Creation Regained: Biblical Basics for a Reformational Worldview,* 2nd ed. (Grand Rapids: Eerdmans, 2005), 2.

43   "a vision of life and for life": Brian J. Walsh and J. Richard Middleton, *Transforming Vision: Shaping a Christian World View* (Downers Grove, IL: InterVarsity Press, 1984), 31.

49   "They anticipate a coming day, however, in which God's restoration will be complete.": These ideas can be reviewed through the study of these relevant texts: John 1; Romans 5; 2 Corinthians 5; Colossians 1; and Revelation 21.

49   "We live in what has been called the 'already and not yet' of the kingdom of God.": See 1 John 3:1–3, Hebrews 2:7–9, and Philippians 3:12–16.

52   "After a narrow escape from angry Jews in Damascus, Paul journeyed to Jerusalem to meet with the apostles.": See Galatians 1:11–24 as well as Acts 9:19–30.

Chapter 4—A Story-Framed Life

63   "In reading the Bible we are asked to relinquish the tight grip of the world's officially approved stories in order to be embraced solely by God's story. The Bible is better than a book of rules. It is a way of transferring us into a new world, of bringing us, step by step, closer to the Kingdom of God.": Tony Campolo and William Willimon, *The Survival Guide for Christians on Campus: How to Be Students and Disciples at the Same Time* (West Monroe, LA: Howard Publishing, 2002), 45.

66   "Hell is the place where nothing connects to nothing.": T. S. Eliot, *Dante* (New York: Haskell House, 1974).

66   "A good curriculum tells a story and invites students to participate in that story.": Neil Postman, *The End of Education: Redefining the Value of School* (New York: Vintage Books, 1995).

Chapter 5—Fish-Eyed Learning

71   "Even 'insiders'—Christian scholars like Os Guinness, Mark Noll, and George Marsden—have described the evangelical mind as flabby, scandalous, and outrageous.": Os Guinness, *Fit Bodies, Fat Minds: Why Evangelicals Don't Think and What to Do About It* (Grand Rapids: Baker, 1994); Mark A. Noll, *The Scandal of the Evangelical Mind* (Grand Rapids: Eerdmans, 1994); George M. Marsden, *The Outrageous Idea of Christian Scholarship* (New York: Oxford University Press, 1997).

73   "the biblical story is sometimes outlined as Creation, Fall, Redemption, and Consummation.": Albert Wolters, *Creation Regained: Biblical Basics for a Reformational Worldview,* 2nd ed. (Grand Rapids: Eerdmans, 2005).

78   "You can begin now to exercise your Christian mind by getting involved in a Bible study and by reading a few books that will help you develop a Christian perspective.": Come to www.academicfaithfulness.com for more suggestions on books to read.

Chapter 6—Four-i-ed Learning

83   "Everything else in the creation is not the One, and nothing in the creation can function as an ultimate anchor for the things in the creation.": See Roy A. Clouser, *The Myth of Religious Neutrality: An Essay on the*

Hidden Role of Religious Belief in Theories (Notre Dame, IN: University of Notre Dame Press, 1991); Colin E. Gunton, *The One, the Three, and the Many: God, Creation, and the Culture of Modernity* (New York: Cambridge University Press, 1993).

84 "[A distinctive approach to Christian higher education] should be an education that cultivates the creative and active integration of faith and learning, of faith and culture. . . .": Arthur Holmes, *The Idea of a Christian College,* rev. ed. (Grand Rapids: Eerdmans, 1989), 6–7.

85 "According to Holmes, holistic learning helps students 'see things in relationship, to organize ideas into an ordered whole, to be systematic, to work toward a unified understanding.'": Holmes, *The Idea of a Christian College,* 30.

85 "[I]n addressing the issue of globalization, no single discipline will enable students to see the relationships between deforestation and shopping malls, free trade and urban migration, new technologies and street crime, international aid and increased hunger. . . .": Richard Slimbach, "Re-Imagining a Distinctively Christian Liberal Arts Education," in D. Glyer and D. Weeks, *The Liberal Arts in Higher Education* (Lanham, MD: University Press of America, 1998).

93 "A liberated imagination is a prerequisite for facing the future. . . .": J. Richard Middleton and Brian J. Walsh, *Truth Is Stranger Than It Used to Be: Biblical Faith in a Postmodern Age* (Downers Grove, IL: InterVarsity Press, 1995), 192.

Chapter 7—Embodying the Outrageous Idea

108 "One of the most important—and much neglected—ingredients of Christian discipleship is the cultivation of a listening ear. Bad listeners do not make good disciples.": John Stott, *The Contemporary Christian: Applying God's Word to Today's World* (Downers Grove, IL: InterVarsity Press, 1992), 101.

109 "We listen to the Word with humble reverence, anxious to understand it, and resolved to believe and obey what we come to understand. We listen to the world with critical alertness, anxious to understand it too, and resolved not necessarily to believe and obey it, but to sympathize with it and to seek grace to discover how the gospel relates to it.": Stott, *The Contemporary Christian,* 28.

109–10 "Why is economics generally reduced to a quantitative science? What is at stake in the synthesis of music and technology in much contemporary music? . . .": Brian J. Walsh, "Christian + University = ?" in *Cue: The Signal to Begin* (preview issue, 1995, available at www .ccojubilee.org/resources/theology/uniwalsh.html).

Chapter 8—Chutes and Ladders

117 "Kosuke Koyama has written a book called *Three Mile an Hour God: Biblical Reflections*.": Maryknoll, NY: Orbis Books, 1980.

119 "Many brilliant Christian professors are teaching in America's colleges and universities, and more and more they are seeing their work as a professor as a call to profess not only facts within their discipline but also the faith-anchored framework that makes sense of the facts.": Marsden argues for just such a movement in *The Outrageous Idea of Christian Scholarship*.